ST CN 3

D0317683

THANKS A MILLION BIG FELLA

Sam Smyth

174.4 SMY

GRIFFITH COLLEGE CORK
Cove Street,
Sullivan's Quay, Cork
Tel. +353 - 21 - 450 7027
Fax. +353 - 21 - 4507659
www.gcc.ie

GRIFFITH COLLEGE CORK

3 9009 00047407 8

Thanks a Million Big Fella

Sam Smyth

GRIFFITH COLLEGE CORK
Cove Street,
Sullivan's Quay, Cork
Tel. +353 - 21 - 450 7027
Fax. +353 - 21 - 4507659
www.gcc.ie

BLACKWATER PRESS

Editor
Aidan Culhane

Design & Layout
Paula Byrne

ISBN
0 86121 952 X

© 1997 Sam Smyth

Produced in Ireland by
Blackwater Press
c/o Folens Publishers
8 Broomhill Business Park,
Tallaght, Dublin 24.

All rights reserved. No part of this publication may be reproduced or transmitted in any form or by any means electronic, mechanical, photocopying, recording, or otherwise without prior written permission from the Publisher.

This book is sold subject to the conditions that it shall not, by way of trade or otherwise, be lent, re-sold, hired out or otherwise circulated without the Publishers' prior consent in any form or cover other than that in which it is published and without similar conditions including this condition being imposed on the subsequent purchaser.

While considerable effort has been made to locate all holders of copyright material used in this text, we have been unable to trace some of these. Should they wish to contact Blackwater Press, we will be glad to come to some arrangement.

About The Author

Sam Smyth is a columnist with the *Irish Independent* and *Sunday Tribune* newspapers. He writes about a wide range of subjects, including politics and showbusiness, and has reported from the United States, Australia, Africa, the Far East, Europe and the Caribbean. He was born in Belfast and moved to Dublin in 1972.

Dear John: The John MacKay Letters (published by Blackwater Press) a book he co-authored with Michael Nugent, topped the bestseller list in Ireland for seven weeks in 1993/1994. In 1996, he wrote *Riverdance: The Story* (published by Andre Deutsch) a book about the internationally-acclaimed Irish music and dance phenomenon.

He is the only Irish journalist to win the 'Journalist Of The Year' award twice: in 1991 for his investigation of business scandals and his exposure of the payments-to-politicians scandal in 1997. In February 1997, he was voted 'Journalists' Journalist' in a poll of more than 250 journalists working on Irish national newspapers, organised by *In Dublin* magazine.

Contents

'Either a prince spends that which is his own or his subjects' or else that of others. In the first case he ought to be sparing, in the second he ought not to neglect any opportunity for liberality ... because it does not take away your reputation if you squander that of others, but adds to it; it is only squandering your own that injures you.'

From *The Prince*
Niccolo Machiavelli (1469-1527)

Prologue

The room was teeming with some 50 or 60 lawyers, maybe even more media people, and the first 60 members of the public who had stood patiently for hours outside in a queue. Nearly everybody was out of their seat chattering excitedly in expectation of the main event. Few noticed as four men entered by a little-used door at the side of the room.

His solicitor led the way, threading an unobtrusive path through the crowd. He stuck close behind, followed by his son and brother. Two seats, just half a dozen paces from the witness stand, were reserved in advance. Charles Haughey moved into the chair beside the aisle and his son Conor sat beside him; Jock, his brother, took a seat in the public gallery behind them, and the solicitor, Michael O'Connor, slipped into his place beside the legal team at the other side of the room.

Charles Haughey's face was a study of disdain and inscrutability, a pose which he had perfected over four decades in public life, designed to ensure he betrayed no inappropriate emotion at an inconvenient time. It served him well waiting for the arrival of the tribunal chairman. He stared straight ahead, ignored an anxious signal from Jock, occasionally turned to his son and whispered a few words; he could have been just another spectator in the public gallery. As news of his arrival was passed from one to another, people strained their eyes searching the room for him, but the slate-grey suit, striped shirt and sober blue tie were useful camouflage. Although he was somewhat older than most, he didn't look much different from the others in a room full of lawyers and professional men in uniformly dark lounge suits, crisp shirts and quiet ties.

His arch-enemy over four decades, Conor Cruise O'Brien, even older and more frail than Haughey, was there, notebook in hand, to savour the ritual humiliation of his adversary. Through a long and distinguished career in journalism, O'Brien had depicted Haughey as the epitome of evil in Irish public life, whose political death he would not believe unless he was buried at a crossroads with a stake through his heart. Jim Dwyer, a Pulitzer Prize-winning columnist from the *Daily News* in New York, scribbled: 'Haughey is seventy-one years old now, with a big beak of a nose, joyless eyes under hooded lids, a mouth that rarely smiles and often curls.' In the media feeding frenzy, the feminist writer Nell McCafferty, a small woman with an affection for him, couldn't see from her seat and stood up to observe every nuance.

The public had begun queuing in the courtyard of Dublin Castle at 2 a.m for this elaborate political and legal pageant. The first in line was a man who would only identify himself as 'a staunch Fianna Fáiler'. By prior arrangement, Charles Haughey was driven through the back gates at 7.20 a.m., avoiding the reporters and photographers waiting at the main entrance and thus scoring his only victory of the day.

The driver of a city-centre-bound bus packed with early morning commuters from Haughey's former constituency on the northside of Dublin, turned up his radio so the passengers could hear the eight o'clock bulletin on RTÉ. The news that Haughey had outfoxed and disappointed the media by arriving early at a back gate drew a spontaneous cheer from the driver and his passengers.

The summit that concluded Ireland's presidency of the EU in 1990 was to be the highest point in Haughey's long career. He had carefully prepared for it for the previous two years. Committees of senior civil servants and government ministers had been instructed to plan every detail. Funds had been allocated to refurbish Dublin Castle. Haughey was determined to impress and lavished hospitality on Margaret Thatcher, Helmut Kohl, François Mitterrand and the other European heads of government. His cavalcade of limousines, flanked by motorcycle outriders, had swept majestically into Dublin Castle by the front entrance. Seven years later, he was slipping in through a back door to avoid potential hostility.

By 8.30 a.m., the crowd at the gate had swollen to a couple of hundred. The first 60 were led to the public gallery in the elegant King George Hall where the tribunal had been sitting for 16 days since April. The overflow was shepherded downstairs, to a large wood-panelled room with deep carpet where some 200 cushioned chairs were arranged in rows in front of two large closed-circuit television screens specially installed to relay the events in the chamber above. When that room was deemed full at 10 a.m., another large room with a single giant television screen was opened to accommodate a further 200.

Writer Liam Fay, who passed on a place in the press room, sat with the overflow. He reported that at least half of the below-stairs public had brought pre-packed sandwiches, and one resourceful couple had an entire four-course breakfast of oranges, bacon rolls, scones and marmalade and tubs of yoghurt which they ate out of a Tupperware bowl. Several hundred people who couldn't gain admittance to the tribunal or its two ante-rooms, waited in the courtyard outside with tiny radios pressed to their ears tuned to news and current affairs programmes. Anyone emerging from the tribunal, was descended upon and asked for details of what was happening inside. A picket organised by the Socialist Workers Party was good-humoured.

Dublin Castle had been the military headquarters and symbol of British rule in Ireland which made it an important setting for the birth of the newly-independent State when the British formally handed over power to the new Provisional Irish government on 17 August 1922. There had been a Dublin Castle on the site since the thirteenth century, where citizens had gathered to witness historic events. Medieval tournaments, where one of the contestants had to die, provided entertainment of sorts in the sixteenth century; there was barbaric torture, long incarceration and political intrigue. But 'the Castle' was also the setting for grand social events where the city's poor would come to gaze at their rulers. Lady Fingal recalled being presented to the Viceroy Lord Spencer as a debutante: 'There was a crowd about the gates of the Castle. The Dublin poor always turned out to see any sight that there was. They shivered on the pavement in their thin, ragged clothes, waiting for hours sometimes, so that they might see the ladies in their silks and satin and furs step from the carriages into the warmth and light and gaiety that received them. The poor were incredibly patient. Even then I was dimly aware of the appalling contrast between their lives and ours, and wondered how long they would remain patient.'

For such an historic event, the Payments to Politicians tribunal was conducted with an admirable informality and an absence of histrionics. There were no wigs or gowns and, mindful of its democratic role, the chairman, a judge of the High Court, Mr Justice Brian McCracken, had benignly indulged, almost encouraged, the public gallery's participation, their regular gasps and occasional spontaneous outbursts of excitement and exasperation. It was the very model of a people's tribunal.

Charles Haughey, a former Taoiseach, would be accused of repeatedly lying; taking secret payments of £1.3 million from the country's biggest retailer, Dunnes Stores, with the consequent questions about whether or not tax had been paid on it; obstructing and delaying the tribunal for six months; and leaving himself open to an enormous potential for bribery and corruption. A former minister and recently re-elected TD for Tipperary North, Michael Lowry, was alleged to have evaded tax on more than £600,000; to have lied to the tribunal; to have misled the Dáil and to have left himself vulnerable to blackmail. It wasn't just the two politicians, but the integrity and reputation of all elected representatives in the Republic of Ireland that was under intense critical scrutiny by the tribunal.

Just after 10.35 a.m., Mr Justice Brian McCracken walked in and everyone in the tribunal chamber stood up. A judicial nod beckoned them to be seated. Counsel for the tribunal, Denis McCullough, a man with a clipped moustache and military bearing, called 'Mister Charles J. Haughey'. The diminutive figure almost glided up the six steps and he carried a buff folder which he put down on a ledge beside the microphone on the witness stand.

It was a summer day in July and outside the sun intermittently broke through clouds. Given the practical demands on the Office of Public Works to hastily construct a makeshift courtroom from an elegant Georgian dining room, it would have been impossible for anyone to better the natural theatrical spotlight which fell on the centre of drama. For just after he took his seat, a single shaft of sunlight beamed through the skylight at a sharp angle and focused directly on the witness box. It bathed Charles J. Haughey in a harsh and blinding light, melting his glacial stare and, just for a moment, appeared to unsettle him. Writer Justine McCarthy noted it was, 'like a biblical painting depicting the ire of a wrathful God'. The registrar, Annette O'Connell, handed him a bible and Charles Haughey placed his hand on it and said, 'I promise to tell the truth, the whole truth and nothing but the truth'.

Chapter One

In 1964, Ben Dunne was coming to terms with his mortality while Charles Haughey was beginning to believe he could walk on water: one preparing to hand on the keys of his retailing kingdom, the other getting ready to leave a footprint on contemporary Irish history. In March that year, at 56 years of age, Ben Dunne created a trust to protect the retailing empire he had created from the tax authorities and any future foolishness by his children. His oldest child, Margaret, had just turned 22 that month, his younger son, Ben Junior celebrated his fourteenth birthday, and the youngest, Therese, was not yet 14. A trust would avoid a massive inheritance tax bill for his children when he died, but more importantly, it would make it much more difficult for the children to sell the company and it should ensure that Dunnes Stores remained a family business.

That same year, Charles Haughey, aged 39, arguably the most talented and innovative Minister for Justice in the history of the State, was tipped as the next Taoiseach. 1964 was a significant milestone on the march toward the age of egalitarianism: Irish workers negotiated a national wage agreement of 12 per cent and a new Labour government was elected in Britain. Both Dunne and Haughey considered themselves class warriors, champions of the working people from whom they emerged. Ben Dunne said he considered himself a purchasing officer for consumers, that he bought goods at the lowest cost and passed on the savings to his customers. Drawing on his own family's experience raising seven children in the 1930s, Haughey would later deliver hefty increases in old age pensions and developed close links with the trade unions. He scoffed at socialism as an answer to the problems of the poor, yet nearly all of the foreign politicians Haughey later admired were of the left: Mitterrand, Schmidt, Delors, Hawke and Gorbachev.

In 1964, 20 years after Ben Dunne opened his first shop in Cork, Dunnes Stores had nine outlets in Dublin alone and an annual turnover of more than £6 million. Dunne believed he had brought nothing less than democracy to retailing in the emerging new Ireland. Haughey had only been elected to the Dáil seven years before, but he had distinguished himself as Minister for Justice for the last three, introducing five major pieces of legislation in 1961, the first year he was appointed. His father-in-law, Sean Lemass, who was Taoiseach, he was a shrewd and plain-talking Dubliner who had built up a strong rapport with Ben Dunne, an equally astute and gravel-voiced northerner, given to even coarser language than his friend in politics.

In the mid-1960s, the sacrifices of the War of Independence, the bitterness of the Civil War, the deprivation of the 1930s and the legacy of the Economic War with Britain were still fresh memories for Dunne and Lemass, both of whom had a vision of a more affluent, modern Ireland. In 1964, the rest of the world was reeling from the shock of the news. The Vatican Council discussed 'the pill' and, after 1,964 years, absolved the Jewish people from guilt in the crucifixion of Christ; Lyndon Johnson was elected President of the United States; Nikita Khrushchev was ousted from power and erased from the history of the Soviet Union; China exploded a nuclear bomb; there was conflict in Cyprus, Laos, Vietnam, the Congo and Malaysia. At home, thousands of Orangemen at separate rallies approved a resolution welcoming 'every opportunity for genuine friendship with our Catholic countrymen'; TDs and Senators voted themselves a wage increase; President de Valera celebrated his eighty-second birthday and Brendan Behan died. 1964 was also the year that Ben Dunne sought commercial immortality and Charlie Haughey took over as Minister for Agriculture.

* * *

Both the Bens, Senior and Junior, must have inherited their penchant for homilies and nuggets of folk wisdom from Barney Dunn. Old Ben's father was something of a Renaissance man, he was a poet, an auctioneer and the bon viveur of teashop society in Rostrevor, a picturesque village tucked below the Mourne Mountains, in south Co. Down. He inherited a café on the quay, the Woodside Restaurant Temperance Refreshment Rooms, and an auctioneering firm which had been established by his family in the late nineteenth century.

A consummate performer, Barney Dunn held court in his café, where he recited his poetry, told stories and did Charlie Chaplin impressions for the tourists who came to visit the local attraction, the Rock of Cloughmore. One of these, Margaret Byrne from Kilkenny, met Barney Dunn at the café and became his wife. Barney had a weakness for alcohol which would wreak tragedy among their descendants, but Margaret was made of sterner stuff and started a drapery business before going on to open a shipping agency which sent many northern Irish emigrants to Australia and New Zealand.

They had three children: Annie, in 1906, Bernard (Ben) in 1908 and Denis born in 1909. Single-minded even as a child, young Ben was wary of his father's drinking and wayward tendencies. While his siblings were playing with friends, his mother gave him a corner of her shop where he repaired bicycles and mended punctures. He had no time for small talk and showed no interest in sport at St Mary's school which he left at 14. Barney Dunn spoke to Johnny Parr, a farm manager with the Rosses of Bladensburg, a local family of landed gentry, and young Ben became a bootboy. Using the savings he had accumulated repairing bicycles and selling berries he picked with his brother, Denis, he bought five sheep from Parr which he kept on a hill with Parr's flock.

While his father was more of an entertainer than an entrepreneur, Ben had inherited a talent for business from his mother and decided to go to America. A friend of his father's, Edward Whittaker, whose own son T.K. would later reshape the Irish economy and write Ben's obituary, managed the Greenmount and Boyne Linen Company in Rostrevor, and talked him in to taking a job as a draper's apprentice in Drogheda. Ben sold the sheep to fund his new life and when he took up his position in Andersons of Drogheda, an 'e' had been added to his surname. Ben Dunne was on his way.

* * *

The working-class Protestants in south Co. Derry never had much material wealth but took comfort in the Union with Britain. Their Catholic neighbours had marginally less means and no consolation for forfeiting their nationalist aspirations. In the early years of this century, Swatragh was nearly as remote from Belfast as it was from Dublin: both unionists and nationalists, like the Haugheys, eked out a living from an unforgiving land, and their religious differences marked down two remarkably similar peoples for separate development.

The Easter Rising of 1916 ignited Sean Haughey's imagination and the inherited dream of an independent Ireland: the O hEochaidh clan traced their origins back to the Uí Néill, Kings of Ulster. For a 17-year-old Catholic nationalist in Swatragh, Co. Derry, joining the Volunteers was nothing less than a patriotic imperative. Sarah McWilliams' family also lived in Swatragh for generations and shared the Haugheys' Catholic nationalism and became involved in the War of Independence. Her family's attachment to the Republican movement continued after the civil war and a brother, Pat McWilliams, was interned in Belfast during the Second World War.

Sarah McWilliams became close to Sean Haughey who was listed as vice-OC of the Second Battalion (South Derry) Brigade of the Irish Volunteers. In a longhand note of a meeting between Michael Collins and the Northern IRA at Portobello Barracks on 2 August 1922, he was described as Brigade OC of the Second Northern Division. During the truce, he was in training at the Curragh where he was ordered to remain when the Civil War began. He married Sarah and in March 1923 he was appointed Commandant of the 61st Battalion, was posted to Ballina, and then to Castlebar.

Their second son, Charles, known in the family as Cathal, was born in Castlebar on 16 September 1925. He had an older brother, Sean, two younger brothers, Padraig, known as Jock, and Eoghan, who became an Oblate priest; there were three sisters, Bride, Maureen and Eithne. A strong-willed man, Sean Haughey resigned from the army after a disagreement in March 1928. He stayed temporarily in Sutton and then moved to a 100 acre farm, the Riggins, in Dunshaughlin, Co. Meath, where the older children, including young Cathal, began their education at infant school in Cushentown and spent long summer holidays back in Swatragh.

In the early 1930s, Sean Haughey suffered ill health and he found it increasingly difficult to cope with farm work. The depression in the US and Europe had made it nearly impossible for a fit man to survive in farming in Ireland and his physical condition was deteriorating. He sold the farm and moved to 12 Belton Park in Donnycarney, north Dublin. Medical diagnosis was an even less exact science in the early 1930s and before his death, Sean Haughey's debilitating illness was eventually identified as multiple sclerosis. His family had to survive on their father's pittance of an army pension and an even smaller IRA pension to which Sarah McWilliams was entitled. Young Cathal, known as Charlie to his new-found friends in Dublin, was enrolled at Scoil Mhuire on Griffith Avenue, and was soon playing on their junior football team. His teachers agreed that Charlie Haughey was an exceptional pupil and in 1938 he won a scholarship to St Joseph's Christian Brothers School, Fairview, acknowledged as the city's northside centre of excellence for talented young scholars of modest background.

'Joeys', as it was known, catered for the cleverer northside boys who believed they were more intelligent, more street-wise and better at sport than what they saw as their more pampered and effete contemporaries on the city's southside. It was the boot camp for the first generation of the post-independence working class preparing to break down the social barriers that had traditionally kept them in their place. In the late 1930s, Joeys was a useful place for what would later be known as networking, or making influential contacts for later in life. George Colley and Harry Boland, one the son of a TD, the other the son of a Fianna Fáil minister, were classmates. Another old boy, Noel Fox who attended 15 years after Haughey, went on to become a trustee of Dunnes Stores, and an intermediary between Ben Dunne Junior, £1.3 million and Charles Haughey.

Besides a grounding in the classics, and a love of poetry in Latin, English and Irish, which he would recite for the rest of his life, young Haughey was a rugged and competitive Gaelic footballer. He was occasionally sent off the field for his foul language and bad temper, another school habit that would last a lifetime. When he played for Parnells, a local GAA club, he was sidelined in a championship match for striking the linesman. The highlight of his sporting achievements was winning a Dublin Senior Football Championship medal with Parnells in 1945. His attachment to the GAA's ideals meant that even as Taoiseach he refused every invitation from the Irish Rugby Football Union to attend international matches.

In 1940, he joined the Local Defence Force and later transferred to the FCA where he rose to the rank of lieutenant and served until he was elected a TD in 1957. A colleague at the time recalls that Haughey took the FCA seriously. A corporal was drilling a squad of some 30 FCA men, all of them, including Private Haughey, with Lee Enfield rifles on their shoulders. The following Sunday the corporal was missing and Haughey had been mysteriously promoted. The rest of the squad resigned in protest. 'This may have been Charlie's first stroke in official Ireland,' said his colleague.

His school friends envied how he could breeze into an examination after no preparation and take top marks. He sailed through the Leaving Certificate winning another scholarship; if he hadn't, then third-level education would have been impossible in his family's financial circumstances. Later, Haughey would say he considered the priesthood and engineering and only made up his mind what course he would do on his first day at University College Dublin in 1943. He bumped into his old classmate, Harry Boland, in the hall at UCD in Earlsfort Terrace and asked him what he was going to do. Boland said he had already agreed to join his brother Enda's accountancy firm. Haughey phoned Enda

Boland at his new accountancy practice from the porter's office, and he agreed that young Charles could join the firm when he finished college. The phone call decided it, and Charles Haughey began a degree course in commerce.

There was no stopping the scholarship boy from the northside. He was elected Auditor of the Commerce Society and elected as the commerce students' delegate on the Student's Representative Council. He regularly debated at the Literary and Historical Society and became immersed in student life. The same year he won his senior football medal with Parnells, he joined a counter-demonstration of UCD students on VE Day in May 1945, and burned a Union Jack which had been raised on a flagpole by students at Trinity College.

Maureen Lemass was one of the 30 students in the commerce class with Haughey and Boland. Charles Haughey began dating his classmate, whom he had known socially for a couple of years. After graduating from UCD in 1946 with an Honours B. Comm, he and his friend, Harry Boland, joined Boland Burke Accountants, in Dawson Street. His father, Sean, died a year later after a long illness and former IRA comrades formed a guard of honour at his funeral. Haughey had no apparent interest in politics until he was asked to join a Fianna Fáil cumann by George Colley and Harry Boland in 1948. In 1946, he became an Associate Member of the Institute of Chartered Accountants and a Fellow (FCA) in 1955. In the Michaelmas Term in 1949, Charles Haughey was called to the Bar.

In 1950, Haughey and Harry Boland set up their own accountancy practice. It was an ambitious move. The profession was dominated by long-established practices, mostly owned by Protestants and so-called 'Castle Catholics', and the moribund economy of the early 1950s made it virtually impossible for newcomers, no matter how ambitious or talented, to get a client base.

It was at Maureen Lemass' twenty-first birthday party in the Country Shop, a restaurant on St Stephen's Green, that he met her father, Sean Lemass, who at that time was the Managing Director of the Irish Press. By the time he married Maureen in 1951, he had become close friends with her father, who was by then Minister for Industry and Commerce. The newlyweds set up home in a neat semi-detached house in Cill Éanna, Raheny, in north Dublin and Haughey and Boland commuted to their offices on the top floor of 13 Dame Street on bicycles. Their first articled clerk was Des Traynor and their second was Maurice O'Kelly, both of whom would later become the joint managing directors of Guinness & Mahon Bank, in the mid-1970s.

After George Colley whetted his appetite for politics, Haughey first stood for the Dáil in the Dublin North East constituency in the general election of 1951 and finished bottom of the Fianna Fáil list with 1,629 first preference votes. He tried again in 1954, and again in 1956, at a by-election caused by the death of Alfie Byrne, but he was poised for success. It came the next year, in 1957, when he knocked out the sitting Fianna Fáil TD, Harry Colley, his friend's father, although it played no part in later enmity between them. It was three more years before he entered government and he was appointed Parliamentary Secretary to the Minister for Justice, Oscar Traynor, who was also his constituency colleague. Later, Haughey said the position was offered to him by Sean Lemass, who said: 'As Taoiseach, it is my duty to offer you the post of the Parliamentary Secretary and as your father-in-law I am advising you not to take it.' He accepted without hesitation.

* * *

Apprentice drapers worked five and a half days a week and his terms of indenture meant Ben Dunne didn't get paid for the first three months he worked in Anderson's Drapery in West Street, Drogheda. The parsimonious philosophy of his new employers was drilled into him daily: 'People who work to spend have nothing, people who work to save have something.' Through hard work and promotion, he hiked up his earnings to 50 shillings a week and, heeding his employer's advice, he saved 12 of these. Later, Andersons would become a branch of Dunnes Stores.

He moved to Cameron's drapery shop in Longford and then at the height of the Depression in the mid-1930s, took up a job in Roches Stores in Cork as a buyer. He met Nora Malone, the millinery buyer in Roches, and they married after several months. There are several versions of his leaving Roches Stores: one that he left after a manager complained that he was earning more in commission than his salary; another, that he decided he should be profiting personally from his own skills as a buyer. Whatever the reason, in 1944 he joined a friend from the north, Des Darrer, and they leased a premises and opened a drapery shop with a staff of 12 across the road from Roches Stores. Huge advertising slogans and advertisements in *The Cork Examiner* newspaper attracted a big crowd on opening day and when the doors opened a window was smashed by the crush of people.

The gardaí were called to control the crowds flocking to buy goods at pre-war prices in the grim days of rationing in 1944. A second shop was opened on North Main Street in 1947, and two more a year later, in Waterford and Mallow. Ben Dunne insisted that the suppliers of goods should stock the shelves in the shop, he piled the goods high and sold them cheap, working on the slenderest of margins. By the end of the 1940s, his mother had moved to Cork to live with his family and in February 1949 he made his last trip back to the North, to bury his father, Barney Dunn, who had lived in Newry for 20 years and died in the workhouse.

The following month Bernard Martin, his fifth child and the fourth Bernard in the family going back to 1835, was born in Cork. Margaret, his first-born had arrived in March 1942; Frank in May 1943; Anne, July 1944; Elizabeth, January 1947; Therese, October 1950. Anne, known to the others as 'the gentle child', suffered an illness when she was 12 and eventually was taken into a residential nursing home in Cork. Conventional family life was a casualty of business success, although it could be argued that Ben Dunne, like successful Asian shopkeepers, saw little difference between business and family life. Eventually, all of them, including his wife, Nora, learned that hard work in the family business was the surest way of winning Ben Senior's approval.

While his rivals in Cork were spending weekends on their yachts, Ben Dunne was holed up in his shops. He passionately believed the consumer is king, that the secret was in the buying and he pushed his suppliers very hard. He said you have to be tough to make people efficient, that goods would be cheaper for the consumer if the suppliers were efficient. Cheaper prices rather than clever salesmanship were the cornerstone of his philosophy. It could be a very confusing philosophy too, he told a competitor: 'I run my business like the Catholic Church ... a very successful organisation. When you tell me the Pope is infallible. You know why? Because the Catholic Church runs the Pope, not the Pope runs the Catholic Church. If he didn't do his job they'd fire him ... and the same thing in Dunnes Stores. I've always made it that Dunnes Stores is the boss, not me.'

His unswerving self-belief continued after he parted from his business partner, Des Darrer, and the onward march of Dunnes Stores continued. Success came at a price. Ben Senior left home on a Monday morning and didn't get back until Saturday night. His wife, Nora, took charge of the Cork stores and was seldom available to her children. In 1954 the fifth store was opened on O'Connell Street, Limerick, and the sixth in Wexford a year later. Crowd scenes similar to Cork in 1944 followed the opening of the first Dublin store in 1958. The first Dunnes superstore on Dublin's George's Street opened in 1960 and was followed by a blitzkrieg advertising campaign: this was a personal choice store with assistants behind every counter – but the customer didn't have to ask for the items, they were on the counter to be felt and examined.

Ben Senior discovered the mark up on fruit and vegetables was very generous and he introduced boxes of apples and oranges in the store at Patrick Street in Cork. He introduced just one more food choice: cream crackers, then had them put in smaller packets and sold with a free portion of cheese. His first own-brand item was a ladies' lumber jacket, available in just one colour, London Tan, sold in its own box for a penny short of a pound and made up for him by Sunbeam, a company based in Cork. It was an enormous success. When staff brought back garments from abroad, they were dissected, colours were chosen and specifications given to a manufacturer who would supply them. The St Bernard brand had a quality control panel which tested the merchandise, ensuring that zips, buttons and quality were of the highest standard. With the luxury of a huge cash flow, Ben Dunne was operating on the principles of banking, delaying payment to his suppliers and earning interest on the money. Low-cost selling meant cutting margins to the minimum but clever management of the cash boosted the profits.

One day in 1965, Ben Senior and his son Frank waded through shoulder-high grass and weeds to inspect two disused factories at Cornelscourt, a heavily-populated commuter suburb south of Dublin. The old man saw retailing as a science, and having watched the growth of suburban retailing in the United States with fascination, he wanted to build the first drive-in shopping centre in Ireland on the site. Stepping between piles of rubble and swooping gulls, he said to his elder son: 'If we can get those birds out, and our birds in, we'll be in business.'

Shopping was becoming a recreational hobby, and when the Cornelscourt Centre opened in 1966, people drove to it from all over the country. Nothing in his life made Ben Dunne so proud as his vast emporium of retailing in south Dublin. A friend said he made no secret of his Holy Trinity of priorities: Business, Religion and Family. He spent more energy and time at business than religion, and family came a poor third, according to a family friend. Old Ben and Nora would often drive out to Cornelscourt on a Saturday, park the car and just watch the throng of customers coming and going without even going into the store.

He never spoke to outsiders about anything other than business and when he became closer to Ben Junior in the late 1960s, the intimacies they traded were all of a commercial nature. There was speculation that Dunnes Stores would seek a stock market listing when the annual turnover was heading toward £10 million. He said: 'I don't want Dunnes to go public. I want to make the Dunne family work. In other words, the Dunnes will have to work for seventeen years or go bankrupt; they're my family ... I think the only hobby I have is work. You can make a hobby out of work, just the same as people make a habit out of worry.'

* * *

Six weeks after his appointment as Minister for Justice in October 1961, Charles Haughey set up a Special Criminal Court staffed by army officers to combat a resurgence of the IRA campaign. Three months later, the IRA announced a ceasefire which effectively ended their border campaign. His determination in dealing with the IRA violence gave him sufficient credibility to entertain his Northern Ireland counterpart, Harry West, at his home in Raheny when he became Minister for Agriculture in 1965. Although his introduction of the farmers' dole, a social welfare payment for smallholders, was a genuinely innovative reform, it was ultimately overshadowed by his continuing confrontations with farming organisations. Mob scenes of protesting farmers would effectively kill off his chances of the Fianna Fáil leadership when Sean Lemass retired in 1966.

Haughey's steely determination to stand by unpopular decisions in his early career was a quality which he was later to suspend and it cost him dearly. As the dreary 1950s gave way to the optimistic 1960s, Haughey, flanked by his two friends and fellow ministers and looking over his shoulder at the country's most go-ahead retailer, was determined to pull a reluctant Ireland into the modern world.

Chapter Two

In 1997, a cult hit film, *Swingers*, and a spin off book, paid a wry homage to the Rat Pack, Frank Sinatra and his buddies, who defined male-bonding and urban sophistication from the late 1950s. They reflected the glamour of their pal John F. Kennedy and his presidency in their expensively-tailored shiny suits and the Rat Pack put hedonism on the agenda for self-made men everywhere. Sinatra and his pals designated Las Vegas as their spiritual home and mirrored the values of the Nevada gambling resort in their bourbon and party-girl lifestyle. In this world where everybody smoked non-tipped cigarettes and drank hard liquor, Sinatra was the link between the mafia, Hollywood and Washington.

Young men with a common purpose read about the Rat Pack in newspapers and magazines, but films like *Oceans 11*, made in 1960, must have held a particular fascination for a trio of like-minded young men in Ireland. The film, which starred Sinatra, Peter Lawford and Dean Martin, was set in Las Vegas. In one scene, Sinatra suggests he buy out the Miss Universe pageant, 'and just sit around and talk to the girls.'

'Why buy what you could get for free?' says Peter Lawford, who in real life had married a Kennedy. The key, Lawford's character, says is, '... turning money into power ... think I'll buy me some votes and go into politics.'

In the early 1960s, Charles Haughey, Brian Lenihan and Donogh O'Malley, young politicians recently elected to the Dáil and aching with ambition, swaggered around Dublin like princes of the city. Later, the most gifted journalist of his generation, John Healy, described them as The Three Musketeers: all for one and one for all. They emulated the lifestyle, their bespoke-tailored mohair suits had a rat-like sheen. Charles Haughey assumed Frank Sinatra's role as leader of the pack.

Guinness' brewery and Jacobs' biscuit factory were the twin peaks of Irish industry. The State was indigent and emigration spirited away the human surplus of economic failure. The Catholic Church, suspicious of change and reluctant to concede any of its enormous influence to politicians, held the country in a drowning man's grip. Sean Lemass knew Ireland had missed out on the massive reconstruction of Europe in the 1950s following World War Two, and a deeply conservative strain in the civil service and the professions frustrated any notions of radical reform.

As rock 'n' roll and prosperity became symbols of a new age in the United States and Britain, the Republic of Ireland was the poor relation on the western seaboard of Europe. Lemass, and the three young bloods in his administration, imbued with patriotism, were embarrassed that their country was seen as backward from abroad. O'Malley was in charge of the Board of Works and he was determined to take civil servants out of their dingy offices and put them into shiny new ones. The developers built the egg-box office blocks and leased them to the government – buildings that were later seen as ugly, but at the time were modern and a symbol of progress. As Parliamentary Secretary responsible for maritime affairs, Brian Lenihan's problem was that the biggest vessels in the Irish fishing fleet were 56 feet long and rarely moved out of sight of land. He reconstituted the fisheries board by coaxing and cajoling officials to implement the necessary changes, but was ultimately disappointed when Ireland's fishing rights were profligately given away in the negotiations to join the EEC in 1972. Haughey was a brilliant and enlightened Minister for Justice who had fought the establishment to effectively abolish the death penalty, and he prepared the way for the Succession Act which was designed to safeguard the inheritance rights of widows and their children.

Their social milieu seemed to contradict their political aspirations: Haughey, Lenihan and O'Malley delivered free travel for old age pensioners, free secondary education for all the children of the nation and curbed the philistine excesses of the book censors. However they mulled over their egalitarian notions and imaginative plans in the opulence of the Russell Hotel's dining-room, in the fashionable Horseshoe Bar in the Shelbourne, or among the horsey set in the Hibernian Hotel. Both O'Malley and Lenihan came from families which had prospered in business, and while the Haugheys had fallen on hard times, Charles never forgot his father was an army officer who could trace his ancestry back to the Kings of Ulster. They plotted their radical reforms together with the confidence of those born to rule. Their confidence was seen as arrogance by many of the old guard of Fianna Fáil while many frontbenchers in the opposition and the senior ranks of the civil service were deeply suspicious of their playboy lifestyles and wealthy friends.

Their camaraderie and willingness to interpret the rules for their mutual benefit was making their friends uneasy and supplying their opponents with ammunition. On 13 March 1962, a garda stopped Donogh O'Malley's car at the junction of Cavendish Row and O'Connell Street in Dublin and asked him if he had seen the arrow directing the traffic. 'What arrow? I didn't even see the bloody Indians,' replied O'Malley. He was charged with driving under the influence and in June he appeared before one of the 'Haughey Courts', an ordinary District Court which sat either before the journalists arrived in the morning, or after they left in the evening. Haughey was Minister for Justice and permitted an arrangement where a defendant who pleaded guilty could have the case heard when newspaper reporters were not present. O'Malley was fined £25 and had his driving licence suspended for 12 months. John Healy, the editor of the *Evening Mail*, confidant of The Three Musketeers and their Boswell, heard about it and splashed the story on the front page. It created something of a scandal, but there was never a suggestion that charges would be dropped, just that O'Malley might avoid embarrassing publicity. Still, it was a privilege the privileged extended only to their friends and the Haughey Courts were not available to anyone outside their own circle.

Also included in that circle were Arthur Gibney, an architect, and Desmond Greevey an engineer. Sometimes the group met in the Martello Tower in the Intercontinental Hotel, or their other haunts around Dublin. There were also whispers of low standards in high places and rumours of corruption over land speculation and property development which T.K. Whittaker's economic development plan had begun to translate into new office blocks and huge expanses of suburban housing. It was possible for a developer to put a small deposit on a site, secure a lease with a government department as a tenant, get planning permission, then have the deal financed by a bank, complete the building, and reap the guaranteed profits from a gilt-edged tenant. It was a financial version of the theory of perpetual motion.

Their reputations as hell-raisers did nothing to enhance their status as potential leaders of government with the grey beards of their own party and in the civil service establishment. O'Malley was the wild one. He was already famous in Limerick for biting the ear off a night porter and had to pay for the redecoration of several bars after becoming involved in altercations.

The Russell Hotel on St Stephen's Green had the best cooking and the most elegant dining room in Ireland which made it a regular haunt of the Three Musketeers. According to John Healy, their most memorable meal there ended with Donogh O'Malley being barred. They had finished dinner when O'Malley's attention was drawn to two buskers, a woman harpist and a male violinist accompanied by a dog, playing outside the window. O'Malley invited them to join him at the table with the two other ministers and shooed the dog under the table. Later, O'Malley blamed Lenihan for kicking the dog under the table, but at the time all the company heard was the dog growling and then bolting. The dog misjudged his jump and landed in the middle of the lower section of the dessert trolley, sending chocolate mousse and pineapples and kirsch all over the carpet. It caused mayhem in the dining-room, although one American in the corner watched with amusement as O'Malley was asked to pay the bill and leave.

A letter followed from the manager asking O'Malley not to frequent the hotel in future. The amused American was on the staff of *The New Yorker* magazine and wrote a very funny account of the incident. Thrilled at the mention in such a prestigious publication, the manager of the Russell rushed another letter to O'Malley asking him to bring his friends for dinner as a guest of the hotel. Although incidents like that outraged many, they endeared the Three Musketeers to others who saw them as champions of ordinary people who would never get an opportunity to tweak the Establishment's nose.

* * *

Sean Lemass was tired and wanted his successor securely in place before the general election of 1966 and when the Taoiseach formally announced his decision to retire, Charles Haughey and his old school friend, George Colley, were the contenders. The choice was stark: Colley, with his flawless Fianna Fáil pedigree, fluency in the Irish language and middle-class respectability, was the candidate favoured by the party's old guard. Haughey, who had proven his intellectual and administrative worth, had also become ostentatiously wealthy, and some feared he would eventually be brought down by scandal. The candidates had not only grown apart, but they had become implacable enemies by the mid-1960s. Haughey was the more clever, resourceful and modern; Colley was dull and stuffy but seemed a safer pair of hands to carry the sacred flame of Fianna Fáil. The leadership contest became so divisive, causing such bitter splits in the party and the cabinet, that Lemass intervened and asked a quiet-spoken barrister from Cork, Jack Lynch, to become a candidate. Haughey, probably on Lemass' advice, withdrew immediately, but Colley insisted on putting it to a vote. Lynch got 52 votes and Colley, 19. As a reward for dropping his candidacy, Lynch appointed Haughey as his Minister for Finance.

Haughey confirmed his reputation as an astute politician and brilliant administrator as Minister for Finance, introducing free travel and electricity, then free television and radio licences for old age pensioners. He reactivated Ireland's application for EEC membership and later introduced a scheme which allowed artists and writers tax-free status. He would be the last Minister for Finance for 25 years to run a surplus on a current budget and cut taxes during his period in office, although his tenure in Finance coincided with economic growth rates of up to ten per cent which gave him the freedom to be bold and imaginative.

The Fianna Fáil young-bloods were devotees of Keynesian economics which had taken the United States out of depression and both the Tories under Harold MacMillan, and Labour's Harold Wilson, applied Keynes' theories to bring prosperity to Britain in the 1960s. Big spenders in their private lives, Haughey, Lenihan and O'Malley also believed in liberally disbursing public money to kick-start the private sector, which led to a race between inflation and growth.

In March 1968, Charles Haughey flew out to open the new Bord Fáilte headquarters in New York. Senator Robert Kennedy, who was running for President, and Cardinal Cushing, the Catholic Primate, were also invited. Haughey had also agreed to officially open an Irish Trade Fair in a Manhattan hotel for the export board, Coras Trachtála. This was the sort of occasion which Haughey relished: an international forum and an opportunity to impress and make friends with important figures who would later be in a position to do favours.

Robert Kennedy, at that time likely to be the next President of the United States, and busy wooing the substantial Irish-American vote in New York, promised to visit the trade fair. Haughey could barely contain his excitement. Waterford Glass, Foxford rugs and an impressive range of Irish craft and produce was on display. Haughey knew one of the exhibitors, Ben Dunne, was a friend of his father-in-law, Sean Lemass, and that fellow Joeys boy, Noel Fox, was one of Dunne's closest financial advisors.

Ben Dunne, a devotee of American marketing and retailing, was a regular at the National Retail Merchants Association conventions and seminars in the United States. He had got the idea of 'self-selection' shops there and two years later, the National Retail Merchants Association honoured him by selecting him for their board of directors. He had invited some of the most senior members of the association to the Irish trade fair where he was promoting his St Bernard label. The most prominent feature on his stand was the latest whiz: the drip-dry,

Bri-nylon shirt. Haughey, whose own shirts were hand made, was horrified and confronted Dunne. 'What do you think this is?' thundered Haughey, 'the fucking Iveagh Market?' It was kind of public humiliation old Ben Dunne regularly dished out to his staff, and even members of his own family. And when Haughey instructed officials of Coras Trachtála to have the Dunnes stand dismantled and taken away immediately, he had made an enemy who would humiliate him even more publicly and more spectacularly, even though it would take another 29 years.

* * *

It was ironic that Ben Dunne's drip-dry, Bri-nylon shirts offended Haughey's developing aesthetic sensitivities. Haughey had been ridiculed as a Donnycarney teddy boy decked out in hunting pink and riding to hounds by the same old-money snobs who believed that Ben Dunne was an irredeemable vulgarian. Certainly Haughey, who had developed a taste for the finer things in life, and had courted the company of artists and writers, would have considered Ben Dunne a social dinosaur and an intellectual pygmy and neither Ben Dunne's money nor his friendship with Sean Lemass intimidated or mesmerised Haughey.

However he was more tolerant and understanding of other men of means who could be just as crude as Ben Dunne. As Minister for Finance he proved his sophistry in economic matters but since the early 1960s he had seemed equally at home in the company of high rollers and their fast money. The resentment and suspicion of the builders and developers he associated with attached itself to the ambitious young minister. Rumours of corruption were widespread as new office blocks and developments in Dublin followed the first flush of affluence. His arch rival for the party leadership, George Colley, pointed his finger at Haughey when he told a Fianna Fáil youth conference in Galway not to be 'dispirited if some people in high places appear to have low standards.' At the time, a shrewd Kerry-born property developer, John Byrne, Ken O'Reilly-Hyland, chairman of Burmah-Castrol (Ireland) as well as a property developer and a fund-raiser for Fianna Fáil, were frequently seen with Haughey. And he claimed Matt Gallagher, of the Gallagher Group, as a friend.

Since the early 1960s, ten years after he had first been taken on as Charles Haughey's articled clerk at Haughey Boland, Des Traynor had taken responsibility for his former boss's financial affairs. He had been made a partner at Haughey Boland on the same day he qualified and shared many of Haughey's personality traits. He was bright, witty, forceful, ruthless, tough, determined to make money and he bought a big house. A family man, who eventually had six children, he neither smoked nor drank, although he took a glass of wine later in life. Later, a former colleague at Haughey Boland described him as 'very manipulative, greedy and avaricious.' While writing *The Destruction Of Dublin*, published in 1985, the author, Frank McDonald, had described Des Traynor as 'Charles J. Haughey's bagman'. Fearful of libel when Traynor was alive, the publisher's lawyers changed the description to 'close personal friend and financial adviser'.

Haughey surrendered the management of his finances to Traynor. He has not had a bank account in his own name since 1961. Traynor had authority to negotiate loans on his behalf without consulting him and never discussed in detail the arrangements he made to deal with Haughey's money problems. Later, one source said Haughey only looked at personal financial transactions when they had more than five noughts: above £100,000. This astonishing arrangement allowed Haughey to live like a fabulously wealthy aristocrat and focus his full attention on national and international affairs without distraction. When Traynor became a hugely successful banker and chairman of one of the country's biggest public companies, CRH, he still took the time and trouble to personally ensure that Charles Haughey had no financial worries. It was also an indication of the respect, and in come cases, awe, in which Haughey was held by many substantial figures in the highest business and financial circles.

For 30 years, Traynor was a director in developer John Byrne's key companies, Carlisle Trust and Dublin City Estates, where he was suspected of representing Haughey's interests. Frank McDonald reported that Byrne's property empire had its headquarters in the Cayman Islands and its accounts in Guinness & Mahon, the bank of which Des Traynor was chairman. In the 1960s, Byrne's office developments, on some of the most prestigious sites in Dublin were an aesthetic blot on the skyline. Buildings such as O'Connell Bridge House, D'Olier House, and Parnell House are monuments to the era of the gombeen man. In 1968, a company set up by Ken O'Reilly-Hyland, called Marlborough Holdings, developed Telephone House in Marlborough Street. Traynor was also a director of the company and Haughey was widely suspected of having a financial involvement.

Haughey's involvement as Minister for Finance with the late Matt Gallagher, and later his son Patrick, also sparked off a flurry of rumours and suspicions. In 1969, the Gallagher Group embarked on an ambitious series of land purchases in some of the most expensive areas in and around Dublin. They snapped up the Watson site in Killiney, 120 acres in Lucan and the Ballally land in Dundrum from which eventually rose 550 houses. Matt Gallagher also negotiated a package deal with Dublin County Council to provide houses of more than 1,000 square foot for £3,250 with loans readily available from the Irish Permanent Building Society. Not one of the sites cost Gallagher more than £2,500 an acre.

In 1971, the Gallagher Group was given planning permission for 3,200 houses, they were building around 550 houses a year and selling another 250 sites a year through another of its companies, Merchant Banking. It was a developer's dream: the builders could barely keep up with public demand and they were amassing a huge land bank. It is little wonder that Matt Gallagher didn't discourage people from calling him 'the man with the Midas touch'. Later, he would praise Charles Haughey's help and encouragement in the development of the Gallagher Group.

A solicitor acting for Haughey denied he had any involvement in a land deal in Harold's Cross in Dublin, involving a four acre site. The Greenmount site, as it was known, was sold by Burmah-Castrol (Ireland), when Ken O'Reilly-Hyland was chairman, to a company called Echo Holdings Ltd, where Haughey's solicitor and election agent, Pat O'Connor, and his son, Michael, were the only directors. In 1975, Echo Holdings got planning permission for office development. Before it was sold on in April 1982, a company associated with Guinness Mahon where Des Traynor was chairman, MS Nominees, replaced the O'Connors as directors. Another director of MS Nominees was Sam Field-Corbett, a partner with Haughey Boland and also a director in the only two companies directly associated with Haughey: Abbeville Ltd, the company which purchased his house; and Larchfield Securities, used to buy Inishvickillane.

In 1983, Haughey's lawyer, Pat O'Connor, wrote: 'Neither Mr Haughey, any member of his family, or body corporate on his behalf have at any time, directly or indirectly, had any interest in Echo Holdings Ltd.' The letter went on to say that to suggest otherwise, would allege that in April 1982, 'while holding the office of Taoiseach' Haughey had 'engaged in a secret business transaction involving the commercial sale of land and profited from that sale as the alleged beneficial owner.'

It was against this background of suspicion and rumour that Fianna Fáil launched Taca, a fund-raising support group of businessmen invited to join and contribute £100 a year to party funds. Haughey was one of the authors of the plan which stipulated that the money was to be deposited in a bank until election time and the interest used to pay for dinners where cabinet ministers would mingle with their benefactors. The American-style fund-raising attracted most of the property developers who were associated with Haughey which prompted questions in the Dáil from the opposition. Although such fund-raising lunches and dinners are now common, at the time they linked Fianna Fáil, and Charles Haughey in particular, to questionable practices.

On the night of 20 September 1968, Haughey sustained serious injuries in a car accident in Co. Wicklow and, while the circumstances were never explained, a directive was given to garda drivers that they were not to allow anyone, including their designated ministers, to drive their cars.

His innovative scheme in the 1969 Budget to allow artists and writers to live tax free in Ireland was over-shadowed by Haughey's mysterious absence. The Taoiseach, Jack Lynch, told the Dáil that the Minister for Finance was in hospital following a riding accident that morning and read the budget address himself. Rumours reverberated around the Dáil, then Dublin and soon the country was engulfed in lurid gossip of how Haughey had been injured. The Garda Commissioner informed the Secretary of the Department of Justice that 'a strange rumour was circulating in north Co. Dublin that Mr Haughey's accident occurred in a licensed premises on the previous night.' The Secretary passed the message to the Taoiseach, but Mr Lynch 'was emphatic' that there should be no garda inquiry into the incident. The most popular story involved a jealous husband, and Haughey, exasperated by the rumours, asked one of his stablehands to speak to the press to confirm that he had witnessed the accident.

In the middle of the general election in 1969, Haughey was at the centre of yet another controversy when it was revealed that he sold his house, Grangemore, on its 45 acres of land, to the Gallagher Group. He bought Abbeville, a magnificent Georgian house on 250 acres in Kinsealy, north Co. Dublin. Built for the Rt Hon. John Beresford, with a Gandon extension added on in 1790, the dining-room was described as 'Gandon's finest surviving domestic interior'. The grand old two-storey house had been on the market for a long time before Haughey bought it, complete with equally magnificent period furniture, for £120,000. He sold Grangemore to the Gallagher Group for £204,000 for development, which enraged his detractors. Conor Cruise O'Brien, who was running in the same constituency, raised it as an issue during the election campaign, denouncing 'the Fianna Fáil speculator-oriented oligarchy'.

Haughey topped the poll in the June election and Fianna Fáil won 75 seats, giving them an overall working majority of five. Two years later,

Cement Roadstone approached Haughey for 'a field' they wanted on the edge of his 250 acres at Abbeville. He sold it to them for £130,000 and more than recouped his outlay on the house and estate. Although he used it to entertain foreign dignatories, Abbeville was essentially a family home. Through the week, Haughey would occasionally spend nights in places that had seen better days, but the weekends at Abbeville with his wife, daughter and three sons were sacred. One close friend said, 'Whatever he did all week, he was an attentive husband and loving father, entertaining personal friends at home or in restaurants nearby.'

As the 1960s were coming to a close, his reputation as an imaginative and innovative minister was copperfastened by his performance in the Department of Finance. However gossip about Charles Haughey's private life and persistent rumours about his personal finances had taken root like a malignant tumour that would grow over the next three decades.

* * *

In hindsight, everything that followed seemed inevitable after the Unionist government in Northern Ireland banned a civil rights march in Derry on 5 October 1968. RUC officers batoned the peaceful demonstrators indiscriminately in full view of the world's press and television cameras. Sectarian violence followed the confrontations between the police and civil rights activists through the summer of 1969 as the Unionist government and the RUC lost control of the streets. Nationalists attacked the Apprentice Boys parade in Derry on 12 August 1969 and the RUC laid a siege on the Bogside area of the city. The rioting spread to Belfast and the RUC could no longer contain the violence in either city. Loyalist mobs followed RUC armoured vehicles into nationalist areas of Belfast and set fire to streets of houses in the Ardoyne and Falls Road. The cabinet met in Dublin and the Taoiseach, Jack Lynch, addressed the nation on television. 'The Stormont government evidently is no longer in control of the situation, which is the inevitable outcome of policies pursued for decades by them,' said Lynch. 'The Government of Ireland can no longer stand by.'

British troops were flown into Northern Ireland to prevent further bloodshed and loss of life. The nationalist communities in Northern Ireland believed they were under siege and vulnerable to further attacks. They formed citizen defence committees and appealed to Dublin for arms. The Minister for Finance in Dublin was sympathetic and later Charles Haughey explained, 'there was a feeling among the government, and among the community as a whole, that we could not do a great deal to help the people of the North. We knew that a lot of people were suffering very severe hardship and distress and the government decided to be generous in coming to their aid. I was appointed as the person to see that this aid was given as freely and generously as possible.' It was an appointment he would bitterly regret.

GRIFFITH COLLEGE CORK
Cove Street,
Sullivan's Quay, Cork.
Tel. +353 - 21 - 450 7027
Fax. +353 - 21 - 4507659
www.gcc.ie

Chapter Three

Like his father before him, Ben Dunne was never posh. Unlike his daddy, he was always rich. From his birth in March 1949 he was swaddled in the trappings of wealth, but as the fifth of six children, his busy parents couldn't afford the time to pay him a lot of attention. When he was still an infant, the Dunnes moved from the neat semi-detatched world of one of Cork's first suburbs, Brownington Park in Douglas, to an altogether more grand detached house in Blackrock.

It was more than a leap of faith. The footloose, fast-buck Dunnes had abseiled into the old-money community of Cork's merchant princes and if the families who had grown rich retailing in Cork for generations found them aggressive rivals on Patrick Street, they must have dreaded them as new neighbours in blue chip Blackrock. Dunnes' pile-'em-high-and-sell-'em-cheap sales pitch had unsettled their genteel competitors who were more accustomed to discreet clients with charge accounts than budget-conscious bargain hunters on a feel-and-buy mission. Once upon a time the grandees could leave the teeming masses on Patrick Street and retreat to their stately piles in the green belt but the arrival of the Dunnes in Blackrock would be a constant reminder of the retailing revolution raging around their stores in the city centre. It was the early 1950s, when hillbilly rock 'n' rollers were ready to topple suave crooners from the top of the pop charts and supermarkets were poised to make a lot of blue-stocking shop assistants redundant.

Barnstead was a fine house built on several acres of land where Ben's older brother, Frank, kept a pony, and the younger Dunnes, except Ben, developed a love of horses that would stay with them all their lives. It was just across the road from St Michael's Church. As a family, the Dunnes, never neglected their religious obligations: their parents went to Mass every day and the family said the Rosary at night. The Dunnes kept very much to themselves, they didn't have the time for the conventions of polite society and were not particularly interested in the social milieu of uppercrust Cork. The Dunnes dealt with the world on their terms. Although they lived in a fine house on a grand spread of land, they were really living above the shop. Both parents were absorbed in the stores and family life was relegated to a neglected branch of the business. Young Ben's first crisis came at the age of two, when he bit through an electric cable in the house and had to be rushed to hospital with burns and shock.

Ben Junior was enrolled at the Presentation Brothers College, favoured by the well-to-do, and one of Cork's most prestigious schools. A big boy for his age, he disappointed some of his teachers who thought that his size might be an indication of a talent for rugby for which the school had a national reputation. They were to be disappointed again. Certainly he showed no interest in, nor an aptitude for, the most basic academic subjects. Neither did he make close friends nor socialise much with his fellow students. The Dunne children never seemed to bring their friends home to their house after school, at weekends, or in the long holidays. Classmates remember him as quiet and gentle which seemed at odds with his size, and strangers expected such a big lad to be bad-tempered and aggressive. But he wasn't: Ben was an agreeable lad and eager to please.

When he was ten, he was rushed to hospital again, suffering a broken leg after falling off his brother Frank's pony, Planet. When he tells friends about growing up in Cork, Ben Dunne now prefers to recall stories which paint a picture of a budding entrepreneur's derring-do, of how he pulled off great trades and deals by inherited, and intuitive, shrewdness. His father was an austere figure whom young Ben could only admire from a distance. From the time Ben was nine years old, his father spent six days a week in Dublin. On Sunday, the talk in the house would be of sales, prices, turnover, competitors and how to beat them. As an adult, Ben told friends his father was 'firm but fair', or 'very kind, tough and ruthless with a huge heart', which, when decoded from the rosy glow of nostalgia, could be interpreted as 'impatient, gruff but generous'. With his father in Dublin, Nora, his mother, was running the business in Cork. It left the two younger children effectively without their parents, like latchkey kids with servants.

Ben seems to have been a lonely boy, closest to Therese, his younger sister. The four older children were taken off on holiday to the French Riviera by their parents while he and Therese stayed at home with the housekeeper. Therese and Ben would remain close through adolescence and their adult lives. When he moved to the senior school at the Presentation College, he had all but given up on education although his teachers kept trying to instill a little learning in him. Exams were always an embarrassment. The Presentation College graded pupils into As, A1s and Bs. Ben was always bottom of the Bs. He couldn't wait to leave school and while his friends played sport or did homework, Ben skipped off to the family store in Patrick Street to pack shelves where he earned a shilling an hour. Schoolfriends recall that he always seemed to have plenty of money, although, they say, he didn't behave like a spoiled brat.

Teachers remember him as respectful and easy to manage, if totally bored by reading, writing and learning. He just didn't want to be there, although neither did he rebel against authority. His aptitude for maths was confined to adding, subtracting, percentages and multiplying: he had no grasp of abstract concepts. Avoiding rugby became an important feature of his life and when school finished at four o'clock, if he wasn't packing shelves at the family store, he would be chatting up girls and hanging out with friends at the Savoy Cinema. In the winter evenings, he built model aeroplanes and would fly them in the summer holidays. But life with the Dunnes was centred on work and the shops, and from the age of 14, Ben spent most of his free time after school and summer holidays in one of the two family stores in the city.

By this time the family had climbed even further up Cork's social greasy pole and moved to Ringmahon House, a stately residence, on a 100 acre farm near Blackrock. The farm was hard work for a young lad, but a valuable training ground. Ben learned the skills of a dealer buying and selling cattle and sheep in the mart. He maintains that quitting school was one of the happiest days of his life and he began working full-time at 16. His sister Margaret, seven years older, started in the business when she was 14 as a floor-sweeper. Beginning in the hardware department in 1965, he moved on to the perilous world of perishable goods in Fruit and Vegetables. His first car was a Ford Anglia and he drove to dances at Crosshaven, or went to rugby hops around the city. He liked girls, although as a teenager friends remember him with just a couple of steady girlfriends.

Ben Dunne wanted to be like his father. He admired him, although he only knew him as a remote figure and a fearsome boss who would often humiliate him on the shop floor in front of the other employees. He was still a teenager when turnover was £6.9 million, although 95 per cent of the trade was in drapery. The St Bernard logo and a blue-collar slogan, 'Dunnes Stores Better Value Beats Them All' was an important component in their marketing strategy. Dunnes Stores had broken into Dublin, into the heart of the city in Henry Street and, more significantly, followed the exodus of the aspiring lower middle class to their new homes in the suburbs. Their huge complex at Cornelscourt, where the car park was even bigger than the store, brought downtown shopping to the sprawling new housing developments in the commuter belt. When Ben

Junior was 19, he followed his father on working trips to Dublin, leaving Cork every Tuesday and going home to Ringmahon on a Friday in his Triumph 2000 car.

Commuting to Dublin and too busy to set up a home in the city, the Dunnes stripped their family life to a minimum and moved into an hotel. Communication was often through the in-house telephone, and for dinner, mother made reservations. They stayed at the old Jury's hotel in Dame Street where one former member of staff described the young Dunnes as 'room service brats'. A businessman who remembers Ben Junior at Jury's, said when he first arrived in 1967, it was sad to see a teenager living in an impersonal hotel, away from his friends in Cork. Eventually, he made his home in the hotel when Dunnes Stores set up its headquarters in Dublin, taking control of the footwear and menswear divisions.

Tall and blunt, forceful when it was required, Ben Dunne towered over Mary Godwin, a fine-boned and delicately-mannered Aer Lingus flight attendant. At first glance, her solidly middle-class and conventional family background in Kilkenny made her an odd choice for the retailing nomad who lived in hotels like a commercial traveller. Maybe it was her common sense and conventionalism that attracted him: the residents' lounge and room service are not a recipe for personal contentment. Later, Ben Dunne would tell friends his father had low personal esteem, which may account for his brusque dismissal and suspicion of what he saw as snobbery in the manners and conventions of the middle class.

Ben Senior and Nora were protective of their children, and wary that they might become targets for financially, if not socially, ambitious potential partners. Ben Dunne's parents signalled their disapproval by refusing to attend the wedding, just as they had done when his brother Frank had taken a Danish wife a few years before, This, even by the stricter social and religious codes of the time, was harsh and deeply hurtful to their children and their spouses. A friend who was later to figure in times of crisis, Father Dermod McCarthy, married Ben Junior and Mary in a quiet ceremony in a Kildare church in 1972. Mary Godwin was brought up in a very different society to the hurly-burly commercial world of the Dunnes, but her air of fragility was deceiving and she became a formidable figure in her own home. Ben moved to their new house in Castleknock, and when Jury's relocated from the city centre to another site two miles away in Ballsbridge, his parents checked in to the Shelbourne Hotel on St Stephen's Green, just a five minute walk to the company's headquarters. Before arriving at work each morning, his father would have done the Stations of the Cross.

Ben Junior was made a director of Dunnes Stores which was expanding rapidly, and by 1976 had an annual turnover of £75 million. By 1981, it was the seventh largest company in Ireland, with more than 40 branches in the Republic. There were eight outlets in Northern Ireland, taking £15 million at the tills each year. Ben Junior was driving a car to match his new found status: a sleek, black 500 SEL Mercedes. On the morning of Friday, 16 October 1981, Ben Dunne headed north for the opening of a new branch in Portadown. Just south of the border post at Killeen, a green car travelling north suddenly swung across the road forcing Ben Dunne to slam on the brakes of the Mercedes. A lorry driver witnessed the scene with astonishment. Four armed and masked men pulled him out of the Mercedes and frogmarched him to the green car, slipped a black hood over his head and drove south. Two of the gunmen sat on him in the back seat for the short drive to the disused old building where he was told to lie on the floor. He gave them telephone numbers for his wife and father and some hours later was marched across fields, then driven to another building where he was forced to remain hooded and lie on the floor.

He didn't know if he would live or die, although being a Dunne, he suspected they were after money. Hooded all day, his sense of smell became more keen and as the days wore on he became sickened by his own body odour. Whether it was the Provisional IRA, or a maverick group of Provos on a private fund-raising operation was, and is, a moot point. The British and Irish governments and the security forces on each side of the border saw the kidnapping as humiliating and an outrageously provocative attack on their authority. The Dunnes had been dealing all their lives but this time they were asked to trade their younger son for £500,000 in used banknotes. The gang had made contact with the family through go-betweens and on the Sunday, Father Dermod McCarthy, met secretly with masked men in Co. Louth and gave them a note for Ben Junior.

Noel Fox, a confidant of Ben Senior, and a trustee of the family fortune, was intercepted delivering money at an hotel near Dundalk, although it was later claimed he was a decoy and another driver eventually delivered the cash. However when it was put to him that he was instrumental in securing Ben Dunne's release, Fox replied, under oath, 'that is correct'. The gardaí had foiled four attempts to pay the ransom but the Dunnes ignored the government's pleas not to trade with the kidnappers. Father McCarthy made an appeal to the kidnappers on radio on the Wednesday; maybe there was a code word in his message. That evening, the London-based soccer team, Spurs, were playing Dundalk in a European Cup match and cars were bumper to bumper on the roads north and south of Dundalk as the security forces checked each vehicle.

Still hooded after six days, Ben was taken from the house, put in the back of a car, and released shortly before midnight at the gates of St Michael's Church in Cullyhanna, south Armagh. Before they drove away, his kidnappers gave him three bullets, two from an Armalite rifle, another from a handgun: one from each of the weapons his captors used to guard their prize. Dunne ran into the graveyard and climbed into a grave which had been opened for a funeral the next day. A radio reporter in Belfast, Eamon Maillie, had been tipped off that Dunne would be in the area and he drove to Cullyhanna. Maillie stopped the car and shouted Dunne's name and then he saw him in the shadows. Both of them called at the parochial house and Father Hugh O'Neill allowed Ben Dunne to telephone an intermediary in Dublin.

A ransom had already been paid. It was no more likely that an IRA group would release Ben Dunne without the ransom being paid, than a shopper would be allowed to leave Dunnes Stores without paying their bill. Dunne sat in front of the fire in the parochial house, drank a bottle of McArdles ale and then sat in the front passenger seat of Maillie's car for the drive south.

A line of gardaí fanned across the road at the border checkpoint in Drumbilla, on the main Dundalk to Armagh road. Maillie asked Dunne what he wanted to do. 'I want to get home', said Dunne. A torch was shone into the car, and the garda asked the routine questions: where where they coming from, where were they going to? He didn't examine Maillie's passenger, the most sought-after man in Ireland, and told them to go on. 'There's a boy for demotion, if ever there was a boy for demotion', quipped Dunne, whose droll sense of humour had returned remarkably quickly after his terrifying ordeal.

He didn't phone his wife, Mary, until they were on the Dublin side of Drogheda, a half-hour drive from home. The family have always denied that any ransom had been paid. However, it was subsequently reported that £350,000 was handed over, although security sources claimed £500,000 sterling, in used bank notes, was passed to the kidnappers in Northern Ireland. In September 1997, a source close to Ben Dunne Junior confirmed a ransom had been paid. Ben Senior, always deeply suspicious of the media, was horrified by the publicity generated by the kidnapping. His son, a chip off the old block, avoided counselling and took just one day off work. He was back in his office on the Friday morning. Dunnes workers, politicians and members of the public filled the Pro-Cathederal in Dublin for a special mass to celebrate Ben Junior's deliverance from evil and return to the power and glory of Dunnes Stores.

Ben Dunne Senior was 74 when the family was faced with the trauma of Ben Junior's kidnapping. Both the British and Irish governments were adamant that no ransom would be paid and the police on each side of the border attempted to seal off the area in south Armagh where they believed young Ben was being held. Their stance didn't matter to old Ben Dunne: there was no question of not paying the ransom, just the practicalities of handing it over to be arranged. Noel Fox had been delegated to secure young Ben's release and discharged his responsibility, with assistance from Father Dermod McCarthy.

It all must have been a surreal exercise in crisis management for Ben Dunne Senior, and his wife, Nora, who continued to live in a bedroom at the Shelbourne Hotel, depending on a hotel staff, whom they rarely tipped, for home comforts. Every morning the couple would order a half bottle of Lanson Champagne and two measures of the syrupy liqueur, green chartreuse. Ben Senior was disliked by the hotel staff: one evening in the dining-room he asked the waiter what was sole bonne femme: 'sole cooked in a white wine sauce with mashed potato piped around and browned under a salamander', he was told. Old Ben decided to order it, but after the first mouthful, he asked for tomato ketchup.

Some days, the old man would leave the hotel and wander around to the company's headquarters for an hour or so. Less and less often he would call into different shops around the city unannounced and unexpected. Long-serving staff would stiffen when they saw him. 'He was intensely disliked', said one Dunnes veteran. 'We lived in fear of him. Anybody that worked with him would recall how he used to shout and roar. All he had was money, he had nothing else of value to offer.' Yet he had done many charitable acts, helped many worthy causes and needy people, but he never wanted any credit or recognition. He seemed to confuse kindness with weakness and would have hated to be thought of as an easy touch. And on a more practical level, old Ben believed he would be swamped with begging letters and hard luck stories if he got a reputation for generosity. The very idea of popularity and glad-handing was alien to him: he gave better value in his stores, and would be judged by that.

Young Ben was taking more responsibility in the business and for the first time in his life, spending time with, and getting to know, his father. They got on really well, according to young Ben who saw how his father operated up close while the grumpy old man explained his peculiar logic.

His father scorned education too, saying that sending a youngster to college to do a commerce degree would spoil any latent talent they might have for business. The daily sermons of toughness, diligence and thrift instilled in him as a boy were now repeated to him as a man.

A decade before, the old man had given an extraordinary interview detailing his folksy and eccentric philosophy. He told Andrew Whittaker of *The Irish Times*, 'I don't think there's any future for companies except they want to be making money. The day for having men on boards that won't be taking a personal interest and be there 24 hours a day is gone. To be on the main board of Dunnes Stores you've got to be on call 24 hours a day and seven days a week. I think the worst thing in this country is top personnel are not working. They're bringing in consultants to look at a company, but the first thing you should look at in a company is the director.' Ben Dunne Senior said he saw no difference going into the Common Market than going into Northern Ireland. 'There's nothing to be afraid of in this world, only understood,' he said. 'When people talk about the economy in Ireland, so little puts it wrong, but so little puts it right ... when I used to go out and play football in my young days, I used to turn round and say to a fellow who was afraid, "do you want to get hurt?" The next thing, I saw him lying down, and he'd be gone off to the pavilion. I did the team a good job because he was yellow ... but when he said, "do you want to get killed?", that was a good man on the opposition team. I tried to keep away from him. You can pass laws that put people out of business, but you can't pass a law that keeps bad people in business.'

It was the first time Ben Dunne Senior talked about himself and his ideas in public, and he never did it again. It was a remarkably frank interview and all the more revealing because the journalist didn't paraphrase his awkward language or try to soften the impact of his harsh words. 'If there's one thing I hate, it's publicity. No one's allowed to write about Ben Dunne. For anyone could have done what I did, but they didn't do it, that's the only difference. The two people I don't like are the people who talk about what they've done and the people who talk about what they're going to do. No one could have done what I did on their own; a good organisation did it. I could see no reason why an Irishman couldn't do what was done in every other country. When people are looking at what you're doing, you're winning. I was down in Florida some years ago and I saw an advertisement for an undertaker that said "Willie Snuffit -- the man who makes dying a pleasure." He did a big business. For success you want to have three things: imagination, determination, and common sense. And if you haven't common sense you don't want the other two. What is common sense to me could be all bull to you.'

Later, Ben Junior would often speak of himself in the third person and repeat similar homespun philosophy to explain himself to others. The fourth generation Bernard had unconsciously inherited a lot from his father, although he was more affectionate and closer to his own children than his father was to him and his siblings.

Ben Dunne Junior had a wife, four children, a tax-efficient mortgage, and an unquenchable ambition when his father died in the intensive care unit of St Vincent's hospital in Dublin in April 1983, two weeks after suffering a heart attack. Government ministers, the Garda Commissioner, bankers, businessmen and sports personalities attended the Requiem Mass at the Pro-Cathederal in Dublin and the funeral procession to Glasnevin cemetery.

T.K. Whittaker, who had done so much to bring prosperity to post-independence Ireland, was the son of Edward Whittaker from Rostrevor who had persuaded the young Ben Senior to take a job in Andersons of Drogheda and not to go to America more than 50 years before. He wrote an appreciation in *The Irish Times* which showed another side to the old ogre. 'Ben Dunne may have been thought a hard man,' wrote Whittaker, 'but those who knew him well saw his soft and charitable side. He preferred to do good by stealth – partly no doubt for the sound business reason that he did not want to invite any wasps to the honey pot ... I had only to vouch for a good cause and he would almost let me write the cheque.' Whittaker concluded, 'Ireland has greatly benefited from his unflagging enterprise and his loss is a national one as well as being a private grief to his wife and family ...'.

When the old man died, there were 48 stores in the Republic, ten in the Cassidy chain, 18 in Northern Ireland and one in Spain, with a total annual turnover of some £300 million. Ben Junior became joint managing director with his brother Frank, and his sisters, Margaret Heffernan, Elizabeth McMahon and Therese Dunne were directors. Frank Dunne had his own difficulties and left Ben in charge. Ben threw most, but not all, of his energies into his work. In the next ten years, turnover rose to some £850 million, there were 88 stores in Ireland, seven in England and two in Spain.

Besides golf, Ben had developed an interest in other leisure activities which would have horrified his puritanical father. In the late 1980s, he began an affair with the estranged wife of an entertainer. He was said to have a grudge against her husband and his own marriage was going through a difficult patch. He was seen in nightclubs, frequently eating late in George's Bistro, a basement restaurant in Dublin, with the woman who was considerably younger. She kept company with a set in Dublin which used cocaine as their recreational drug of choice and sources close to Ben Dunne have since confirmed that she introduced him to it. Cocaine, the most expensive and exotic of the illegal drugs, also has its own rituals and protocols, and the idea of sniffing it through a rolled up £100 note, undoubtedly appealed to him. The expense and exclusivity was one attraction, but the exhilarating effect and the sense of confidence it instilled in the big awkward man, must also have made it a powerful compulsion. Although it is not physically addictive, cocaine users rapidly develop a psychological dependence. Ben Dunne always dominated any company he was in and the euphoric effect of the narcotic, levelling his inhibitions and inflating his ego, encouraged him to talk non-stop. He rapidly developed a serious habit. The woman had ready access to cocaine dealers and Ben Dunne was one of the richest men in Ireland: it was a combination destined to end in disaster.

Chapter Four

Charles Haughey's legacy is littered with sins of omission and 'if onlys'. Most of his own regrets, and the disappointments of his supporters, are a result of actions he failed to take or things he didn't do. Since 1970, his record is blotted with indecisiveness and failures of courage which contradict his earlier promise and achievements. There are many sins of commission on his record too, a few of them bold decisions which ended as honourable failures. His early political career is studded with bold initiatives and imaginative leaps taken against the paralysing advice of conventional wisdom. As Minister for Justice, and immediately after as Minister for Finance, he showed rare flashes of vision and occasional flourishes of courage. But despite his obvious administrative abilities and a natural flair for the art of politics, the gossip and rumour that plagued his personal and political life made even some of his most ardent admirers uneasy even before 1970.

However he had underpinned his popularity in Fianna Fáil after securing an overall majority with his performance as Director of Elections in 1969, when his indefatigable confidence struck a chord with the public. In that era of can-do optimism, Haughey was seen as go-getter. He was also more of a loner. The era of The Three Musketeers ended with the death of Donogh O'Malley in 1968 and Haughey was no longer as close to Brian Lenihan. If much of the fun had gone out of politics, it did nothing to blunt his ambition. He was still widely admired and seen as the man most likely to succeed. Such great expectations for his undisputed talents made his fall from grace in May 1970 all the more sensational. His sacking from the government and then his arrest and trial for allegedly conspiring to import illegal arms, really did live up to the tired old cliche of 'rocking the State to its foundations'.

Few contemporary critics can fully understand the backdrop of near anarchy and the murderous attacks on nationalists on the streets of Belfast and Derry which led to Haughey's appearance in the dock. But then Charles Haughey didn't trust himself, or a Dublin jury, to put his own actions, and those of his fellow accused, in context either. It was the ultimate test of character: he had two choices, although they were far from simple. He could take the high road, tell the truth and live with the consequences; or he could choose the low road, lie, and hope to eventually salvage his career. Whether it was overweening pride or moral cowardice which motivated the perjury he offered as evidence to the court, is a moot point. Although he couldn't have known it at the time, if he had told the truth, it wouldn't have changed the outcome of the trial. He would still have been acquitted and been one of the few to emerge with honour from the fog of ambivalence, lies and half-truths which characterised the Fianna Fáil government of the day.

The other three defendants, Captain James Kelly, an Irish Army intelligence officer; John Kelly, the OC of the Provisional IRA in Belfast; and Albert Luykx, a Belgian businessman living in Dublin, admitted they had attempted to import arms, but claimed it had been implicitly sanctioned by the Minister for Defence, Jim Gibbons. However, it wasn't enough for them to show they had government approval to import arms, their legal defence required them to prove the arms were for the use of the Irish defence forces.

The prosecution hoped to prove that the army weren't paying for the weapons; that the arms were not being imported through conventional military channels; that the arms were not to be stored in an official military premises; that the intention was to load the arms on to a civilian lorry at the point of importation; that part of a consignment of bulletproof vests which did get through, did not go to the Defence Forces.

The circumstances leading to the trial highlighted the confusion and ambivalence of the Irish government faced with the violence in Northern Ireland in August 1969. The nationalist areas and Catholics of Belfast had come under sustained attack from loyalist mobs and rogue elements of the RUC and B Specials. There were genuine fears of pogroms and in response, the Irish army was training young men from Derry in the use of weapons, under cover as members of the FCA, at an army camp in Co. Donegal. Refugee camps were established in the Republic to shelter mostly women and children escaping from the violence in the North.

In October 1969, 15 old Republicans, travelling as members of defence committees, met Captain James Kelly in Bailieborough, Co. Cavan. They discussed setting up a Northern Command of the IRA which would not operate in the Republic. As Minister for Finance, Charles Haughey, authorised a payment of £100,000 to a bank in Baggot Street in Dublin to establish a Fund for the Relief of Distress in Northern Ireland. £60,000 of this money was spent by John Kelly, the Officer Commanding the Provisional IRA in Belfast: £30,000 went on arms and £30,000 on IRA wages. Kelly and Jock Haughey, a brother of the Minister for Finance, arranged to purchase arms in London through another government minister, Neil Blaney, which turned out to be a trap laid by British Intelligence.

In December 1969, Kelly and the Provisional IRA leader in Derry, Sean Keenan, went to purchase arms in New York which were to be paid for from the bank account in Baggot Street, Dublin. IRA men travelled to Vienna to meet another arms dealer and arrangements were made for fishing boats to rendezvous with a freighter from Hamburg at the Kish lighthouse near Dublin and bring the arms ashore. That deal, which had been set up by Albert Luykx at the hotel he owned in Sutton, Co. Dublin, also fell through. Haughey arranged customs clearance for the importation of arms at Dublin docks on 25 March 1970 and at Dublin Airport on 18 April 1970. His cabinet colleague, Kevin Boland, said Haughey informed him in early March 1970 about the proposals to import arms. Captain Kelly gave evidence to both the court and the Dáil Committee of Public Accounts that he had told Haughey of the plans to import arms in Februry 1970. The Secretary at the Department of Justice, Peter Berry, said he had informed the Taoiseach in his office about the involvement of two ministers in the attempts to import arms on 13 April 1970, although Jack Lynch subsequently denied this.

Neil Blaney and Kevin Boland were known to be deeply sympathetic to militant Republicanism, but Haughey's smashing of the IRA border campaign when he was Minister for Justice just eight years before, made his involvement in the plot more puzzling. When his father-in-law, Sean Lemass, was Taoiseach, he had met the Prime Minister of Northern Ireland, Terence O'Neill, at Stormont on 14 January 1965 in an attempt to ease the mutual suspicion and hostility over partition. A month later, Haughey had entertained the Northern Ireland Minister of Agriculture, Harry West, at his home in Dublin. And his father had joined the pro-Treaty forces as a commissioned officer in the Irish Army which had opposed militant Republicanism. Still, Haughey had spent many of his summer holidays as a child in south Co. Derry and his mother's family there were implacable opponents of Unionism.

Regular contacts with the murky world of arms dealing meant it was only a matter of time before the attempts to procure arms in Europe came to the attention of intelligence services. It is believed that British intelligence informed the Special Branch in Dublin about the plan to import arms. Jack Lynch was preparing the ground to seek Blaney's and Haughey's resignations. Haughey was in the Mater Hospital in Dublin after the accident on Budget Day when the Taoiseach told the cabinet at a meeting on 1 May 1970 that allegations had been made against two cabinet ministers purported to be involved in a conspiracy to illegally import arms. The allegations had been denied and the matter seemed to be closed.

Liam Cosgrave, the leader of Fine Gael, had been informed of the details by Special Branch officers and rather than raise it with Lynch, he tried to leak it to a newspaper. Ned Murphy, who covered the Dáil for the *Irish Independent*, didn't run with the story and Cosgrave approached Lynch on the evening of 5 May and officially informed him about the alleged conspiracy of two government ministers to import arms. The Taoiseach asked Blaney for his resignation, he refused, then Lynch sacked him – and Haughey. Kevin Boland resigned in protest. Charges against Blaney were thrown out in the District Court on 2 July when his counsel, Liam Hamilton, submitted that there was no case to answer.

Every day was like a theatrical first night while the Arms Trial sat in the Four Courts. The acrid smell of stale tobacco smoke was overcome by the whiff of expensive perfume as the serene and beautiful Hilda O'Malley, the young widow of Donogh O'Malley, made an entrance. She wore equally glamorous clothes, a tapestry-patterned maxi dress and big, round blue-tinted glasses framed by long blonde tresses. Each day, Albert Luykx, accompanied by his in-laws, had smiles for everyone. Captain Kelly's wife, in a neat grey two-piece suit attended each day with their two beautiful red-haired daughters. John Kelly, the Provisional IRA commander in Belfast, could have been a solicitor's clerk with his unfailingly courteous manner and his sober suit. Charles Haughey, always well-groomed and sleek, arrived separately with his friend and solicitor, Pat O'Connor.

In court, four witnesses, including his co-defendant, Captain James Kelly, who said he had put him 'fully in the picture' in February, gave evidence that Haughey knew about the plot to import arms. Haughey's personal assistant, Tony Fagan, maintained he had informed Mr Haughey on 19 March 1970 that Captain Kelly had sought customs clearance for a consignment which, Kelly said, the minister would know all about. Peter Berry said that Haughey had guaranteed him the arms consignment would go directly to the North if it was allowed through. The Minister for Defence, Jim Gibbons, gave evidence that Haughey told him he would have the operation called off for a month at a meeting in his office on 30 April 1970. Haughey denied all of the evidence, including the testimony of the four witnesses. His own evidence was that even if he had known that the consignment was of arms, he would still have authorised customs clearance for it because he would have understood it to be an operation directed by army intelligence acting on official orders.

In his summing up to the all-male jury, Mr Justice Henchy highlighted the conflict of evidence between two government ministers, Charles Haughey and Jim Gibbons. 'Now I regret to say, gentlemen, that it seems to me, and I think it will seem to you, in regard to the conversation which Mr Gibbons said took place in Mr Haughey's office on Friday the 17th of April, or Monday the 20th of April, either took place or it didn't take place. Either Mr Gibbons, it seems to me, has concocted – invented as counsel put it to him – this conversation, or it happened in substance. As you will see later, Mr Haughey denies it and he cannot explain how his former colleague could say it is so. It is not like something said in the course of a conversation that could be misrepresented. It seemed to me, and you are free to dismiss my opinion, either Mr Gibbons has concocted this and has come to court and perjured himself, or it happened. If there is another explanation, please act on it. There does not seem to me to be any way of avoiding the total confict on this issue between Mr Haughey and Mr Gibbons.'

As Kevin Boland later wrote, the acquittals in the arms trial do not imply that the jury accepted the evidence given in the case by Charles Haughey. As the other three defendants were also acquitted, and as their defence was that the attempted arms importation was not illegal, then on that basis Mr Haughey would also would have had to have been acquitted, irrespective of whether the jury believed what he said in evidence. Mr Haughey's defence of not knowing anything about the attempted arms importation, and of having no involvement in it, was irrelevant once the jury decided there was at least a reasonable doubt about the illegality of the operation.

The Taoiseach, Jack Lynch, was making a speech which included more conciliatory policies on Northern Ireland at the United Nations in New York on Friday, 23 October 1970, when the jury acquitted the four defendants.There were wild scenes outside the Four Courts and Haughey called a press conference where he challenged Lynch's leadership and claimed his United Nations speech was not Fianna Fáil policy. 'Those reponsible for this debacle have no option open to them but to take the honourable course open to them. I think there is some dissatisfaction about the leadership at the moment. The Taoiseach's position is something that will be decided by the parliamentary party,' said Haughey, surrounded by supporters, including a businessman from Longford, Albert Reynolds, who had followed him from the Four Courts. When Lynch disembarked from the aircraft at Dublin the following

Monday morning, every government minister, except two who were out of the country, turned up to greet him with more than 50 TDs and 27 senators and senior party figures.

Lynch promised further investigations into the allegations and the Dáil Committee of Public Accounts discovered that money from the Department of Finance had been transferred through the Irish Red Cross to bank accounts in fictitious names and that part of it had gone to Northern Ireland for the purchase of weapons. Haughey vehemently denied to the committee that he knew anything about Captain James Kelly's purchase of arms, and that the Fund for the Relief of Distress in Northern Ireland, which was funded by his department, would have been totally inappropriate for such a purpose. His brother, Jock, denied under oath that he had controlled one of the accounts, but refused to answer any other questions. He was convicted of contempt and sentenced to six months imprisonment by the High Court, but appealed successfully to the Supreme Court which overturned the conviction on the grounds he might incriminate himself.

Lynch said there could not be even the slightest suspicion about the activities of a minister, although there was difficulty reconciling Jim Gibbons' testimony in court and the answer to a question he gave in the Dáil. 'I wish emphatically to deny any such knowledge' (of the proposed importation of arms), he told the Dáil. Although in court, Gibbons admitted that Captain Kelly *had* informed him. In a vote of censure in the Dáil, Kevin Boland resigned from the Dáil rather than vote confidence in Gibbons. Haughey had no such reservations or scruples in supporting Gibbons, just as he had voted confidence in the Taoiseach and his government just weeks before. In a statement issued before the vote on Gibbons, he said, 'The time has come to leave the events of May 1970 and their sequel behind us and let history judge all who played their part in them.'

His friendship with his co-defendant, John Kelly, a senior figure in the Provisional IRA, continued and he described Kelly as 'the finest Republican it has been my privilege to know.' Through 1971, his association with well-known Republicans was monitored by the Special Branch who kept surveillance on his house and tapped his telephone. If anything, the scandal of the arms crisis had strengthened support for him.

Haughey reinvented himself as a Renaissance man in an address titled 'Art and the Majority' at the Harvard Summer School in July 1972. In a superbly-crafted speech, he spoke about the State's role in the arts and defended his own decision to allow artists and writers tax exemption. What would old Ben Dunne have made of his assertion that 'the Prince of Salzburg supported Mozart right enough, but clearly there was no love lost between them'. Or his reference to Michelangelo, 'whatever the relationship between the painter and the Pope, when it came to the ceiling of the Sistine chapel, the painter was the more important of the two.' Written by his friend, the poet Anthony Cronin, the speech maintained that much of theatre and orchestral performances underwritten by governments subsidised the performing artists and audiences at the expense of creative artists. He also received a signal that he was not as isolated in the party as his opponents hoped: he was re-elected honorary vice-president of Fianna Fáil at the Ard Fheis in 1972.

He had drawn the proverbial line in the sand, and the Arms Trial and the crisis of 1970 were no longer discussed, or even mentioned, in his company. His principal opponents, George Colley, the Taoiseach's economic adviser, Martin O'Donoghue, and the Minister for Justice, Des O'Malley, were effectively running the party with Jack Lynch. They negotiated entry to the EEC and repaired the damage done to Anglo-Irish relations by the arms crisis. Haughey took to wooing the Fianna Fáil party faithful in the country. At least three nights nearly every week, he drove to party meetings around the country with a young admirer, PJ Mara. They took turns behind the wheel and discussed the leadership of the party or the people they met at functions. It was a long way from the candlelit dinners in Dublin's better restaurants and hotels and the wealthy businessmen with whom he regularly associated.

Haughey developed a close relationship with key figures in the Fianna Fáil organisation around the country, building a national network of supporters which by-passed the party headquarters in Dublin. The lamentable performance of the government gave him an ideal platform to strut his stuff before the grassroots, although he avoided overtly criticising his former colleagues. He was a now a more cynical and calculating man which, combined with an equally determined and ambitious political drive, made Haughey a formidable figure.

In February 1973, Fianna Fáil went into opposition after the general election and Haughey was elected chairman of the newly-formed Oireachtas Joint Committee on the Secondary Legislation of the European Communities in July. He was on the way back, but he was travelling alone. The Three Musketeers of the previous decade were little more than a fading memory. Although he was away from the centre of power, Haughey continued to rise at six in the morning and paid for a special delivery of his post which allowed him to deal with his correspondence and be ready to face the day at nine o'clock. His daily work rate was phenomenal, taking care of his business in the Dáil, dealing with constituency matters, often heading to a party function in the country that evening. He continued to live in spendid isolation in gilded comfort, spending the weekends with his family and a coterie of friends.

While the party was castigated for performing badly in opposition, support for Haughey among both the rural and urban working-class party members continued to grow. And after five years languishing on the backbenches, Jack Lynch reappointed him to the front bench, as spokesman on health, in January 1975. As expected, Haughey was supremely competent and confident, although he was despised by the inner circle around Jack Lynch. It was Colley, O'Malley, O'Donoghue and Lynch who masterminded the 1977 general election manifesto which swept Fianna Fáil to government with a record 84 seats. Haughey was appointed Minister for Health and disapproved of the populist giveaway manifesto which abolished car tax and domestic rates. He embarked on a series of gimmicks in his department which were guaranteed to generate publicity and he was determined to distance himself from the looming crisis which their economic policies had made inevitable. George Colley tried to impose a two per cent levy on farmers which led to an unprecedented revolt among Fianna Fáil backbenchers, and his eventual climbdown damaged both himself and the government. Although unemployment had fallen, the price was a climbing wages bill for public employees and government borrowing rose dramatically.

In 1979, Fianna Fáil's vote slumped to just 35 per cent in the election to the European Parliament which panicked many of the TDs elected for the first time. Public spending was spiralling out of control and a strike by postal workers, then long queues at petrol stations following another oil crisis, left Jack Lynch's leadership vulnerable. There was deep dissatisfaction and nervousness within the parliamentary party and a significant faction believed Haughey offered a solution while George Colley was deemed to be part of the problem. Jack Lynch indicated he would resign in January 1980, when Ireland had completed its term as President of the EEC. Colley and O'Donoghue believed Haughey wasn't ready for a leadership contest and persuaded Lynch to announce on 5 December that he was standing down. Liam Cosgrave paid a tribute to him where he described Lynch as 'the most popular Irish politician since Daniel O'Connell'.

Colley's junior minister, Ray MacSharry, proposed Haughey for the leadership. A newly-elected TD from Longford, Albert Reynolds, along with Padraig Flynn, Sean Doherty, and another newcomer, Charlie McCreevy from Kildare, joined Haughey's team. He was elected leader by secret ballot on Friday, 7 December. Haughey expected to win by a comfortable majority, but in the end it was by just six votes – 44 to 38.

Before he was elected Taoiseach, he met Colley who only agreed to serve in his government if he remained as Tanaiste and had a veto over the appointments to the two sensitive security portfolios: Justice and Defence. If only Haughey had had the courage to refuse, many of his later problems may not have arisen. His surrender of authority to appoint his own ministers not only undermined his own position, but was tantamount to accepting that he couldn't be trusted with the security of the State. Haughey believed that if he reappointed most of Lynch's cabinet members, it would help heal the deep divisions in the party. O'Donoghue had already said he wouldn't serve under Haughey, but Gibbons and two others were dropped. He rewarded his friends: Ray MacSharry was appointed Minister for Agriculture, and Albert Reynolds, Minister for Posts and Telegraphs; Maire Geoghegan-Quinn was the first woman since Countess Markievicz to be appointed to cabinet.

On his election as Taoiseach on 11 December, Dr Garret FitzGerald, the leader of Fine Gael, made an uncharacteristic and unprecedented personal attack on Charles Haughey. While his mother, his wife and children were watching from the public gallery in the Dáil, FitzGerald referred to Haughey's 'flawed pedigree' and said his motives could only be judged by God. 'I speak not only for the opposition but for many in Fianna Fáil who may not be free to say what they believe or express their deep fears for the future of this country under the proposed leadership, people who are not free to reveal what they know and what led them to oppose this man with a commitment far beyond the normal ... we cannot ignore the fact that he differs from all his predecessors in that those motives have been and are widely impugned, most notably, but by no means exclusively, by people within his own party, people close to him who have observed his actions for many years and have made their human interim judgement on him .... The feet that will go through that lobby to support his election will include many that will drag; the hearts of many who will climb those stairs before turning left will be heavy. Many of those who may vote for him will be doing so in the belief and hope that they will not have to serve long under a man they do not respect, whom they have fought long and hard, but for the moment in vain, to exclude from the highest office in the land.'

The intense rivalry, mutual distrust and dislike between Haughey and FitzGerald was a metaphor for the antipathy between the two major political parties. Although each recalled the other from their time at University College Dublin, they had virtually nothing in common. Haughey emerged from a poor family on Dublin's less salubrious northside, played GAA and became a success through his own talent, scholarships and the Christian Brothers. FitzGerald's family were of the privileged professional classes on the southside, his father was a minister in the first Free State government, he enjoyed a Jesuit education and his family name alone opened doors everywhere. By some inherited imperative, Haughey, the poor boy from the northside, lived in a magnificent period house, had his complicated finances managed by Des Traynor and received callers on a Saturday morning. His friends were an eclectic bunch, but Haughey was always suspicious of the establishment figures from the professional classes and most of those with whom he socialised were self-made men.

FitzGerald, who was always short of money, lived in faded grandeur in the sort of untidy house favoured by eccentric academics in British films of the Ealing heyday. Bored by materialism, he was drawn to abstract problems and his interests ranged from theology to studying airline schedules. Nothing illustrates the difference between the two former Taoisigh than how they dealt with people in trouble. Even people who didn't like Haughey believed he could solve their problems. Like some old Mafia Don, they visited him, he listened, told them he would see what he could do, but never promised a solution. He could be gruff but they were rarely disappointed.

Garret FitzGerald, a kind man who espoused a more egalitarian approach and enjoyed an unusually close relationship with his wife, had difficulty dealing with the everyday problems that faced folk in less comfortable circumstances. While he could grapple with quantum physics and statistical conundrums, his abstract approach to life left him at a disadvantage dealing with other people's personal and domestic difficulties.

FitzGerald had insulted and humiliated Haughey in the presence of his family on what should have been the happiest day of his life in the Dáil. His friends believed the Fine Gael leader's malice in the 'flawed pedigree' speech was rooted in snobbery and even if he didn't realise it himself, FitzGerald's attack was an affirmation that those who emerged from the working class couldn't be trusted to run the country. Garret FitzGerald later apologised for the remarks, but as he had said – there were also people in Fianna Fáil who agreed with him. Still, nine years after his multiple humiliations, Haughey was Taoiseach while his tormentor was leader of the opposition.

Chapter Five

Maybe Pierce Brosnan should take the title role in the movie, *The Michael Lowry Story*. It would be a sort of log cabin to the White House fable, the kind of film popular with tycoons in the Hollywood of the 1950s, but the Irish farm boy who moves to a mansion and ends up in Government buildings would be a tainted hero, disgraced in the last reel of a morality tale. *The Ethical Death of a Salesman* might be a more appropriate title for an almost Gothic melodrama about an ambitious country boy made good and brought down by greed. Scenes of high farce and hick foolishness, interspersed with a narrative of naive venality, would introduce the froth of soap opera to the darker recesses of Michael Lowry.

He was born in March 1954 in Holycross, Co. Tipperary, to a close-knit family. There were six boys: Jack, Phil, Pat, Ned, Michael, Jimmy; and one sister, Mary. Their father, Mick, was from a neighbouring parish, Drunbane, who left Tipperary, bought a pub in Dublin, sold it, then moved to Mullingar and bought another pub in partnership with a cousin. In 1945 they sold up and he moved back in Holycross where he bought a 160-acre mixed farm.

Although some of his family were Fianna Fáil supporters, Mick Lowry Senior had neither passion nor time for politics, although later he voted for the local Fine Gael TD, Tom Dunne. Like so many men of his generation and background, Mick Lowry's life was devoted to farming and his family. He died in 1971, the year the son who was named after him left school and began work, leaving Esther and son Jack to run the farm. Esther Bourke was also from Drunbane and came from solid Fine Gael stock. It was Esther's politics which dominated, and in Holycross, Lowrys' was known as a staunch Fine Gael house. Like her husband, Esther Lowry's life was centred on the family and the farm. Neighbours described her as 'a lovely, respectable, shy woman who is devoted to her family'.

The Lowrys made a comfortable living from the farm, all the boys attended Holycross National School and later the Christian Brothers School in Thurles. They all did well and still live in, or near, the parish of Holycross. Phil was co-opted on to the county council when Michael was appointed a minister in December 1994 and is a full-time coach with the GAA and a selector of the county's minor hurling team; Ned owns a bar in Bohernacrusha; Jack runs the family farm; Pat runs Michael's refrigeration company, Streamline; Jimmy was in the fast food business; Mary is married and lives near Holycross. All of them canvass for Michael at elections.

Michael Lowry, the fifth son of the family, didn't like school, reserving the passions of boyhood and adolescence for sport. Much of life in the Lowry house revolved around sport and GAA games, particularly hurling, which consumed most of the talk after Mass and in the local pubs in Holycross. His former teachers in CBS Thurles remember Michael as an 'ordinary, pleasant, well-mannered, smartly-turned-out boy'. He had no memorable academic achievements and one teacher recalls him as a 'run-of-the-mill club hurler, a solid hardworking player who took up the less glamorous defensive positions such as corner back; not particularly talented'. He played with the minors, but was never seriously considered for the county team.

Besides sport, Michael Lowry was a keen dancer and with four or five friends packed into a car, borrowed from their parents or elder siblings, they drove to see the popular showbands of the early 1970s at dances in Fermoy and Limerick. Michael Lowry loved the showbands and the dances which were the epicentre of social life for young people in both rural and urban Ireland since the early 1960s. He was a big fan of Dickie Rock and the Miami, Brendan Bowyer and the Royal, Joe Dolan and the Drifters, although he also liked the new British and American rock groups and he described the Beatles as his favourite. A non-smoker, he was a moderate drinker, a bottle of lager was his first choice and as dedicated and disciplined in his work as he was passionate for sport. As a teenager, he had no political affiliations.

Like Ben Dunne, Michael Lowry didn't do the Leaving Certificate. He left the CBS in Thurles at 17 and joined a small firm in the town, Butler Refrigeration, as an apprentice engineer in 1971. There were only four employees based in a garage beside the Butlers' family home and young Lowry proved himself to be a quick learner, a willing worker and eager to please. A year later, as business picked up, the company moved to a new warehouse at Tortulla, Thurles. As the company grew, Butlers secured the contracts to service the refrigeration for the country's biggest retailing chain, Dunnes Stores, and their rivals, Quinnsworth, in the Munster area.

The beginning of a boom in frozen food sales led to an increasing demand for industrial and retail deep freezers. One of Michael Lowry's particular talents was convincing customers to buy new units rather than have older equipment repaired. As business improved, Butlers took on more employees and Michael Lowry moved into sales full-time, eventually persuading Matt Butler, who treated him as a surrogate son, to create a new position for him as sales manager.

They expanded further when another contractor got into financial difficulties and Butlers saved the day by finishing off the refrigeration installation for a new Dunnes premises in Clonmel. More design, layout and installation contracts outside Munster followed after they successfully bid for the contract to supply and install the refrigeration at a new branch of Dunnes Stores in north Dublin. As Dunnes expanded and more branches requiring even more refrigeration were opened over the next ten years, the two companies developed a close working relationship. However Matt Butler, a cautious and independent-minded man, kept their business with Dunnes Stores on a formal footing.

The same talent for sales and organisation that marked him out for promotion in his day job was useful in his ambition for climbing the greasy pole of GAA politics. In Holycross, as in much of rural Ireland, gaelic games were the local passion and took up whatever leisure time was available in the evenings and at weekends. Michael Lowry began to spend nearly as much time involved in the administration of the sport in the evenings as he did training and preparing for Sunday's game. A knee injury in his mid-twenties transferred him permanently from senior club hurling for Holycross to the proverbial smoke-filled rooms of GAA committees. He had found his niche. A diligent administrator and tireless organiser, he put to use his formidable powers of persuasion which had proved so successful selling fridges, convincing other committee members to his point of view.

However his flair for fund-raising gave him a vital extra edge in GAA politics. He volunteered for other time-consuming committees and it paid off later when he was elected Chairman of the Mid-Division of the Tipperary County Board. The internal politics of the GAA was a special forces training academy for anyone drawn to council chambers and party political in-fighting. Doing whatever is necessary to secure a majority, requires exactly the same skills in a sports organisation as a county council or the national parliament.

The town of Borrisoleigh was to play a pivotal role in Michael Lowry's life: his future wife, Catherine McGrath came from the town and it was in

Borrisoleigh where he took his first shaky step into national politics. It was unthinkable that he would join any party other than Fine Gael and he took out membership in the mid-1970s. He joined with David Moloney, a handsome and highly-regarded young solicitor who was subsequently elected to the Senate in 1977, and Tom Berkery, a more cautious man closer to the perception of a solid Fine Gael traditionalist, who would challenge Lowry in a dramatic election more than 20 years later.

The local TD, Tom Dunne, a quiet man who rarely spoke in the Dáil but had a reputation for looking after constituency matters, was a major influence on Michael Lowry. Tom Dunne had a serious car accident and lost his seat when Fianna Fáil swept to an overall majority in the 1977 general election, but he continued to serve as a county councillor. In 1979, the team that looked like running Fine Gael in the area for the next generation, was elected to Tipperary (North Riding) County Council: David Moloney, Michael Lowry, Tom Berkery and Tom Ryan.

Michael O'Kennedy, a Fianna Fáil TD in the constituency, was appointed European Commissioner in 1980 and the prospect of a by-election loomed in Tipperary North. Fine Gael was determined to win back the seat that got away four years earlier and a selection convention was held in a small town in the centre of the constituency, Borrisoleigh, on a cold January night in 1981. Tom Berkery withdrew before the meeting was called to order and two young tigers contested the nomination: David Moloney, 30 years old, and Michael Lowry, 27 years old. The two contenders had an acute geographical problem. One was from Thurles, the other from Holycross, just a couple of miles away. There could only be one candidate from the Thurles/Holycross area and the loser couldn't expect to run for Fine Gael in the foreseeable future. There was speculation that the by-election may never be held, but whoever was selected would go on to fight the next general election in the Fine Gael livery.

When the party leader, Garret FitzGerald, and the National Organiser, Peter Prendergast, turned up at the Marian Hall, all 300 seats were filled, the aisles blocked and the doorway jammed with excited Fine Gaelers. A sense of optimism and a wave of enthusiasm had infected even the more cautious members. Oliver Fogarty from the Thurles District Executive proposed Lowry and reminded the delegates that Lowry was a playing member of Holycross GAA, a director of the Rent-An-Irish Cottage Scheme and had played a crucial role organising the 300 Club Draw. May Quinn proposed David Moloney and pointed out that there were 21 branches and 300 registered members in the party after the 1977 election and since Moloney had taken up the Fine Gael banner, there were now 49 branches and 1,000 registered members. 'David is young and vigorous, with integrity and vision,' said May Quinn.

Gene Kerrigan, who covered the convention for *Magill* magazine, wrote, '... the main difference in style and approach was clearly that in the Moloney camp words like 'indefatigable' came easily to the lips while the Lowry troops were more alert to the political benefits of the Rent-An-Irish-Cottage Scheme.' Lowry had the confident look of a successful salesman; Moloney, the urbane solicitor, carried the distinguishing mark of the professional caste.

More than 500 people spent three hours in a hall licensed for 300, no one switched off the heating and condensation streamed down the walls. Already pale, Michael Lowry's face drained of all colour when the result was announced: 201 to 49. Lowry was gracious in defeat, hid his disappointment, licked his lips and said, 'to be honest, I expected to do a bit better.' He urged supporters to 'use every drop of blood possible in your body to ensure that you get every vote possible for David Moloney.' The two contestants shook hands. Last word went to the National Organiser, Peter Prendergast, who urged the Fine Gael faithful to go off and talk of David Moloney, think of him, dream of him, and when they wake up in the morning they must do so with David Moloney's name on their lips. Just as the more experienced political handlers in Tipperary North suspected, there was no by-election but David Moloney won the seat for Fine Gael in June 1981 and held it again in the general election the following year.

Although he was widely tipped for a place on the front bench, Moloney was unable to run in the 1987 general election because of family commitments. Still, it is a measure of the regard in which he was held within the most senior ranks of the party, that Moloney was appointed National Director of Elections.

Moloney's difficulty was Lowry's opportunity and he organised a formidable campaign for what was essentially a safe Fine Gael seat. He romped home but the running didn't stop after he was elected. While David Moloney had been more cerebral, with a deep interest in national and international affairs, Michael Lowry ran the constituency on the clientelist model laid down by their predecessor, Tom Dunne. He appeared to be shy, he was clumsy with language, he rarely spoke in the Dáil, but Lowry established an extensive network of clinics, championing a cunning combination of traditional ward-warming and modern management techniques. Party workers greeted constituents, took details from them and prepared a brief for Lowry so he would be familiar with their problems when they were ushered into his presence. His solution was passed on to secretaries who would immediately telephone whatever State agency, department or local authority office Lowry believed could help resolve the difficulty. Problems were frequently sorted out before the constituent left the premises. His reputation as an instant solver of problems spread beyond his own area and people from neighbouring constituencies seeking his help came to the network of clinics he organised all over north Tipperary.

After Michael Lowry was elected to the Dáil in May 1987, he could no longer operate as a full-time salesman and struck an arrangement with Matt Butler that allowed him the use of a company car and he was paid commission on any sales he made. Matt Butler was extremely proud when his sales manager was elected to Dáil Éireann and, for the next year and a half, Michael Lowry continued to work part-time for his company.

Many of his backbench colleagues in Leinster House found him dour and taciturn, gauche and awkward. But an appetite for hard work, attention to detail and a willingness to please senior party figures was an ample substitute for urbane sophistication. He found his voice in the Dáil in May 1988, withdrawing in protest when a meeting of the Oireachtas Joint Committee on Commercial State-Sponsored Bodies was convened 'on the eve of a likely election' it was, he said, 'a crude attempt to use the committee for party political purposes'.

That was just a day after he took a traditional Fine Gael line on tax cheats, and objected to the minority Fianna Fáil government's Second Stage of the Forestry Bill. He complained that the government had not taken strong action to stop the black economy thriving in the forestry programme. He said, '... our Forestry Service is an unwitting employer of black economy labour because its contracts for most of its work do not facilitate a proper check on the tax regime of those employed'. Maybe it was Lowry's concern about the black economy that spurred the Fine Gael leader, Alan Dukes, to appoint him a junior spokesman with responsibility for industry and commerce in October 1988.

Chapter Six

In 1966, Charles Haughey told the Dáil he kept 2,000 chickens on his farm in Co. Meath. They all came home to roost over the first three years of the 1980s. His own reckless profligacy with the economy of the nation was matched by the shrinking fortunes of his personal finances. On 10 January 1980, less than a month after he was elected Taoiseach, without a hint of irony or a twinge of embarrassment, he addressed the nation. 'We have been living away beyond our means,' he said with with an undertaker's solemnity. 'We have been living at a rate which is just not justified by the amounts of goods and services we have been producing. To make up the difference we have been borrowing enormous amounts of money, borrowing at a rate which just can't continue.' While Haughey was advocating civic fiscal rectitude, Des Traynor, who managed his personal finances, was making regular calls to the branch of the Allied Irish Bank in Dame Street, negotiating loans and extending overdraft facilities for his client.

Haughey had spent the previous 11 years restoring his eighteenth century mansion, Abbeville, to pristine condition: replacing timbers riddled with dry-rot, renovating the stables and outhouses, repairing the roof; installing central heating, even adding an elaborate fountain beside the driveway. Expensive furniture, oriental rugs, Jack Yeats paintings and a cellar stocked with fine French wines gave Abbeville the ambience of the aristocratic residence it had once been. There were thoroughbred horses gambolling on the 250 acres of land and the only visible income supporting it all for the previous decade was Mr Haughey's annual salary as a TD and the bonus of three years as a government minister.

At the end of 1980, less than a year after his television appeal for national belt-tightening, the economy was in crisis. Garda pay had been underestimated by 30 per cent and the army's by 28 per cent. The social welfare budget was overspent by nearly 45 per cent and there were 110,000 on the dole when provision had only been made for 106,000. This drew attention to another hostage to fortune: Jack Lynch had said back in 1977 that Fianna Fáil didn't deserve to be in government if the dole queues reached 100,000.

And there was seething discontent within the party: just a week after Haughey was elected Taoiseach, his Tanaiste, George Colley, was already chipping away at his authority. Colley, O'Donoghue and O'Malley were convinced Haughey had conceived and planned the downfall of Jack Lynch. It took 12 years for one of the plotters against Lynch to set the record straight. In January 1992, Charlie McCreevy said: 'It is untrue to say that Charles Haughey orchestrated an undermining campaign against Jack Lynch. It is correct that it was pro-Haughey people who participated, but the man himself neither orchestrated nor encouraged it: of course, neither did he do anything to halt it. George and his followers sincerely believed Haughey's treachery in the demise of Jack Lynch, but in this they were wrong. An unfortunate consequence of that period was that the pro-Lynch and Colley axis of the party believed the orchestration theory when their favourite didn't succeed. This was the basis of many of the party's troubles in the early 1980s.'

The assumption by his opponents in the early 1970s that Haughey's fingerprints were on everything and anything undesirable in Ireland, was taken up by a wider audience in the 1980s. No allowance was made for unfortunate coincidence or even bad luck, and he had more than his share of both. But his insecurity as party leader and desperation for popularity distorted his judgement at times and gave credence to his adversaries' view that he wasn't fit to hold high office.

There was only one flash of good news, and that too was imbued with irony. Haughey's meetings with Margaret Thatcher laid the foundations for the Anglo-Irish Agreement in 1985, which was to be Garret FitzGerald's most memorable achievement. Later, Mrs Thatcher could barely bring herself to speak to Haughey when he broke ranks with the other EC countries and accused Britain of being the aggressor in the Falklands war. Haughey had planned on an early election in 1981, but on the opening night of the Ard Fheis, 14 February, a fire in the Stardust discotheque in the heart of his constituency, killed 48 young people. The hunger strikes in the North bitterly divided the country and led to a grim uncertainty before the general election in June.

Before the election was called, Haughey seized control of Fianna Fáil fund-raising from Des Hanafin, a supporter of Jack Lynch, who was very successful in securing money from the business community from his base in the Burlington Hotel. He also replaced Paul MacKay, the treasurer of his constituency organisation, with his long-time friend, solicitor Pat O'Connor. MacKay and Hanafin were deeply suspicious of what they believed was Haughey's hands-on approach to fund-raising. Paul Kavanagh, one of Fianna Fáil's principal fund-raisers from the early 1980s until the early 1990s, disagreed. 'He was the very opposite,' said Kavanagh, an independently wealthy and successful businessman. 'In the ten or eleven years I was doing it, he never once asked me what anyone gave. A number of times I went to discuss it with him, but his hands went up. He didn't want to discuss it.' Denis McCarthy, Roy Donovan, Peter Hanley, Noel Hanlon, Eimear Haughey and Conor Crowley sat on the fund-raising committee with Kavanagh.

In the 1981 election, Garret FitzGerald travelled by coach and his personal election expenses as party leader were reported to be £11,000. Haughey travelled by helicopter, which cost £235 an hour plus ten per cent extra at weekends; his personal expenses ran to £40,000, and he lost. 'Between those three elections in the early 1980s we spent a minimum of £4 million. The budget for one was £1.7 million, it was spend, spend, spend. Dunnes Stores would have been on the computer read-outs and every single person or company on them was written to by Mr Haughey and then we phoned them, arranged to meet them or called around,' recalled Kavanagh, whose integrity was never questioned.

When they took office, Garret FitzGerald's coalition struggled and juggled to demystify the voodoo economics which Haughey had controlled through the medium of his Minister for Finance, Gene FitzGerald. The coalition collapsed when its budget failed to make it through the Dáil in January 1982 and 'The Haughey Factor' made its debut in the subsequent election campaign. Fine Gael's public relations specialists targeted him, and a spate of ugly rumours about Haughey's financial and private life succeeded in stopping Fianna Fáil getting an overall majority. Even before the election for a new Taoiseach, Des O'Malley, Colley and O'Donoghue planned another challenge but it petered out before Haughey was appointed Taoiseach – supported by the votes of the independent Dublin TD, Tony Gregory, and three TDs from the Workers Party. The Fianna Fáil minority government in 1982 lasted just nine months and, like some phantom pregnancy, delivered nothing but pain and disappointment. In a long public life which had many lean years, 1982 was Charles Haughey's *annus horribilis*.

No event that year burned into the public's consciousness more deeply than the Macarthur murders. It was also one episode over which Haughey had no control and he was guilty of little more than the misfortune of being in office at the time. A socially ambitious dilettante, Malcolm Macarthur, callously murdered a nurse, Bridie Gargan, in the Phoenix Park in Dublin, then shot dead a farmer, Donal Dunne, in Edenderry, Co. Offaly. At the time, he was staying at the home of the Attorney General, Patrick Connolly, an apartment overlooking Dublin

Bay, and it was there he was arrested. Some time before, Connolly arranged to visit the United States and while en route was called back.

When it was reported, scurrilous rumours about a homosexual scandal raged around the country. Although Connolly was unmarried, he was heterosexual, even something of a ladies' man, but the absence of hard information fuelled further gossip. The Attorney General flew back to London by Concorde after a call from the Taoiseach, and resigned after arriving in Dublin. At a press conference, Haughey explained the circumstances as grotesque, unbelievable, bizarre and unprecedented. The acronym was harvested by his old adversary Conor Cruise O'Brien, and GUBU became his literary cosh.

It would be difficult to better Haughey's description of the circumstances surrounding the arrest of Macarthur, and only the most biased commentator would lay any blame on the Taoiseach. As the late John Healy wrote, 'If Charlie had ducks, they'd drown on him'. But the blame and hostility that rained down on him were an indication of the intensity of anti-Haughey feeling in the opposition and media at the time. There was worse to follow.

The Avoca Mine in Wicklow had lost £10 million since 1975 and a memorandum to the government on 16 July 1982, advised closing it down and appointing a receiver. On 27 July, the Secretary to the Government, wrote to the Minister for Industry and Energy, Albert Reynolds, advising him to appoint a receiver. Neither the Memorandum for Government nor the government's decision made any recommendation about who should be appointed receiver, although the ICC who represented the government's interests at Avoca, recommended Stokes Kennedy Crowley. A note in the file said that a list of nominees should be sent to the minister for approval, although an earlier memo submitted to Mr Reynolds by Mergers Ltd, suggested three companies: Stokes Kennedy Crowley, Craig Gardner and Coopers & Lybrand.

However, on 6 August 1982, Noel Fox of Oliver Freaney & Company was appointed. Mr Reynolds, who made the appointment, said Fox hadn't been his choice, but 'a government decision', although sources close to Mr Reynolds later said it was the Taoiseach, Charles Haughey, who had insisted on Mr Fox's appointment. In that ill-fated minority government of 1982, Mr Haughey also had his financial adviser, Des Traynor, appointed to the board of Aer Lingus. Haughey hadn't forgotten the old boys in his alma mater. He was still friendly with Noel Fox who had attended St Josephs and trained as an accountant with Haughey Boland. Fox had subsequently become a senior partner in Oliver Freaney

& Company, the auditors for Dunnes Stores, and he was a trustee of the Dunne family trust.

As of November 1997, Noel Fox of Oliver Freaney & Company had been paid a total of £246,381 for fees in respect of the 15 year receivership of Avoca Mines which still hadn't been completed. However, sources at Oliver Freaney maintained it was a particularly complicated receivership and that the vast majority of the fees were incurred in the first few years. On 28 April 1997, an internal Department memorandum stated: 'The Department is pressing the receiver's office and the solicitors for early completion, in conjunction with the Chief State Solicitor's Office. While there are outstanding elements in the receivership, no further fees will be paid to the Receiver.'

Oliver Freaney, a former Dublin GAA football hero, was old Ben Dunne's financial adviser and accountant, and a pal of Charlie Haughey's. When he ran into personal difficulties in the late 1980s, Ben Dunne Junior loaned him £300,000. The bulk of the money was repaid the following year, then he died unexpectedly and the balance was paid after a long drawn-out administration of his probate.

Charlie McCreevy put down a motion of 'no confidence' in the leader before a meeting of the Fianna Fáil parliamentary party in early October 1982. Haughey insisted on absolute loyalty from his cabinet; Colley announced that O'Donoghue and O'Malley would resign from cabinet rather than support the leader. Haughey won by 58 votes to 22, but the mood in Leinster House had turned poisonous. Both McCreevy and Jim Gibbons were jostled, spat upon and had to have a Garda escort to their cars. The incidents were floodlit by television cameras and pictures of the thuggery were broadcast to the country. An opinion poll taken three weeks later showed that only 23 per cent of those polled were satisfied with the government, and Haughey's personal popularity had plunged to 32 per cent. The government collapsed under the weight of its own incompetence and unpopularity a couple of weeks later.

Just a week after Garret FitzGerald was voted in as Taoiseach and the coalition took office in November 1982, Peter Murtagh, the security correspondent of *The Irish Times*, reported that the home telephones of two journalists, Bruce Arnold and Geraldine Kennedy, had been tapped with the full knowledge and approval of Sean Doherty, the previous Minister for Justice. It was a sensational story. It emerged that the official in the department responsible for checking applications for tapping phones, was told by a Garda Deputy Commissioner, Joe Ainsworth, that Arnold was 'anti-national in outlook and might be obtaining information from sources of a similar disposition.' A journalist of the highest integrity and honour, the only reason for tapping Arnold's phone was because of stories he was writing which criticised the Taoiseach. Geraldine Kennedy had written authoritatively about a cabinet meeting held on 11 July 1982 when the government had reversed its economic policies and decided to apply more discipline to exchequer finances. Charles Haughey had tried to discover the source of her information from her employer and failed. Her phone was tapped a few days later.

On 20 January 1983, the new Minister for Justice, Michael Noonan, confirmed the journalists' telephones had been tapped and that the usual procedures and protocols had not been followed. Haughey vehemently denied any knowledge of the phone tapping, but both journalists were subsequently awarded compensation by the courts. The phone tapping scandal led to another no-confidence motion on his leadership of Fianna Fáil and Haughey's chances of survival appeared so slim, the *Irish Press* printed his political obituary. He survived, against all the odds, by 40 votes to 33.

The Forum for a New Ireland was Garret FitzGerald's talking shop to prepare the way for the Anglo-Irish Agreement. All interested parties, from the Republic and Northern Ireland, were invited to discuss the political future of the island at Dublin Castle. The discussions were confidential, but, inevitably, there were leaks to the media. FitzGerald and Haughey complained, but on one occasion the leader of the Labour Party, Dick Spring, accused Fianna Fáil of breaking confidence. Haughey became enraged and demanded that he withdraw the allegation, but Spring refused. Haughey became very emotional and appealed to the rest of the conference, pleading that no one had suffered more from journalists than himself. He couldn't continue, Charles Haughey was visibly distressed, wept aloud and had to be helped from the room.

Opposition was agony for Haughey. Although George Colley had died unexpectedly while undergoing heart surgery, Des O'Malley was still implacably opposed to his leadership. O'Malley lost the whip after speaking in favour of a coalition government bill to legalise the sale of condoms. But when he accused the leader of stifling debate on the report of the Forum for a New Ireland, Haughey immediately moved to have him expelled from the party. O'Malley's demands for a secret ballot were ignored and 73 agreed to his expulsion while only nine dissented in a roll-call vote. In December 1985, he founded the Progressive Democrats with another former Fianna Fáil TD, Mary Harney, and Michael McDowell, the former secretary of Garret FitzGerald's constituency organisation in Dublin South East.

Haughey's personal finances were in crisis. His financial adviser, Des Traynor, had borrowed and negotiated overdrafts worth nearly £1 million with Allied Irish Banks. Interest rates were rising and the bank was becoming increasingly concerned that they had no security to cover their exposure. Haughey's only apparent income was his salary as a TD and ministerial pensions, and the bank put pressure on for the repayment of the debt. He sold off a poultry farm near Ashbourne in Co. Meath which he had owned since the 1960s, but times had changed since the 1960s and early 1970s when money and influence had been more readily convertible currencies. Traynor must have been very concerned.

For more than 20 years Des Traynor had looked after Haughey's finances. He was the first employee at Haughey Boland and articled to Charles Haughey in 1950, and made a partner on the same day he qualified. In the early 1960s, he began organising Haughey's financial affairs, with the authority to borrow and arrange credit without having to get specific authority from, or refer back to, his client. He advised him about the sale of his land at Grangemore to the Gallagher Group for £204,000 and the purchase of Abbeville, which Haughey picked up as a bargain for £120,000. After negotiating a number of property deals with Guinness & Mahon bank in 1969, the chairman, John Guinness, invited him to become a director.

It was a very unusual invitation from a very orthodox bank. Guinness & Mahon were seen as the British establishment in Ireland, and they were the only merchant bank in Ireland until AIB began their investment bank in the late 1960s. Jonathan Guinness, whose wife Jennifer was later kidnapped from their home in Howth and later rescued unharmed by the gardaí, was impressed by Traynor. The other banks in Dublin could only lend money, but as the only merchant bankers in town, Guinness & Mahon could lend money and take part of the equity from the clients. As a risk-taker with a good instinct for business himself, the old British bank and the young ambitious accountant were a formidable combination.

At his first board meeting at Guinness & Mahon's offices in College Green in Dublin in May 1969, two things struck Traynor as odd. The first was that a lot of people, many of them with titles, travelled to the meeting from the United Kingdom. The second was when the silver tea trolley was brought into the board room he was asked, 'Indian or China?' Traynor said, 'China', while everyone else asked for Indian. He learned never to ask for 'China' again. Traynor settled down to a long and successful career, and a year later he became a managing director with Jonathan Guinness and William Forwood, a classical scholar and old Etonian.

It was Traynor who set up a subsidiary in the Cayman Islands, Guinness Mahon Cayman Trust in 1969 and from the mid-1970s, their bank in the Caymans placed substantial deposits in the Dublin headquarters. In May 1976, Traynor was appointed Deputy Chairman of Guinness & Mahon which made him a full-time Chief Executive in Dublin. A small, stocky man who took no exercise and was a heavy smoker, he had a heart attack at the age of 39. Still, he was soon to be chairman of New Ireland Assurance. He was also an adviser to companies owned by some of Haughey's close friends, and a director of John Byrne's Carlisle Trust and Dublin City Estates. Byrne angrily denied suggestions that Haughey had ever secretly owned any part of his companies, although sources say that Traynor and Haughey may have helped secure tenants for developments owned by Byrne's companies. As an accountant trained in the less complicated world of the 1950s, he offered some people apparently simple solutions to the increasingly complex world of the 1980s.

The rumours about Haughey's financial difficulties began circulating around Dublin's banking and business circles in late 1982 and through 1983. Haughey blithely went about his hectic social life: weekends in Paris, his shirts bespoke tailored by Charvet just across from the Ritz in the Place de Vendôme. In Dublin, his favourite restaurant was also the city's most expensive, Le Coq Hardi, where his favourite champagne was Dom Perignon. According to an associate of both Haughey and Traynor, 'his [Haughey's] attitude to money was like the British royal family's: he doesn't care where the money comes from as long as it is available.' Haughey's secretary at Abbeville sent his bills to Haughey Boland and Des Traynor transferred money to the accountants who paid his creditors. The pressure from AIB to regularise overdrafts and loans he had arranged for Haughey, must have added to Traynor's already heavy work schedule.

In the mid-1980s, Haughey told the bank he wasn't in a position to pay off his overdrafts and borrowings, gambling that they would not go ahead with their threats of legal action. Traynor was not as confident as his client and negotiated for the bank to write off some of the debt and discount the balance. Meanwhile, the bills for Abbeville, and the cost of the construction of a house on the island he had purchased off the Kerry coast, Inishvickillane, were mounting. The AIB was owed nearly £1 million. As a banker himself, Traynor knew AIB would rather get some of the money they were owed than take legal action with its consequent hurricane of controversy and publicity. And even if they did sue Haughey, the AIB could still be left empty-handed. Traynor made a deal: the bank would write off some of the money and discount the rest. But the AIB wanted cash and they wanted it quickly.

Ironically, Traynor was dealing with the AIB branch beside the first Haughey Boland offices in Dame Street. He bought Haughey's loan from AIB and took it into Guinness & Mahon. Haughey was given a bank draft for £500,000 and made an arrangement to meet a senior executive at the door of AIB's headquarters in Ballsbridge. The executive was waiting when Haughey's car pulled up and the draft was handed to him dismissively through the open window of the passenger door. 'A gentleman wouldn't have done it', said one banking source.

The coalition had been disintegrating through the second half of 1986 and it was obvious they could not agree a budget in January 1987. They had doubled the national debt, the economy was in crisis and the internal tensions had become intolerable. Taoiseach Garret FitzGerald dissolved the Dáil and called an election for 17 February. Once again Haughey's character was a campaign issue. And when he was elected Taoiseach of a Fianna Fáil minority government in March, he repeated the 1980 mantra and promised to put the economy on a sound footing. Although Fianna Fáil had made extravagant promises in the campaign, Haughey consulted Colm McCarthy, an economist who had been a constant critic of the previous government's irresponsible public spending. Haughey also appointed Ray MacSharry, a serious man with a steely determination, as his Minister for Finance and he brought in Padraig O hUiginn, a wise and wily civil servant, as Secretary to the Department of the Taoiseach.

MacSharry's first budget cut the borrowing requirement of the previous government by one per cent and slashed the budgets of the big spending departments: Social Welfare, Health and Education. Garret FitzGerald resigned as leader of Fine Gael and he was replaced by Alan Dukes who realised the seriousness of the economic crisis. In October, Dukes outlined a strategy of not opposing the government's harsh policies which allowed Haughey some room for manoeuvre. Haughey's performance as Taoiseach, on his third time as head of government, drew almost unanimous praise from former critics. Fianna Fáil and Fine Gael worked closely together to organise the smooth passage of bills through the Oireachtas and, as 1987 came to a close, Alan Dukes gave Haughey an undertaking that he would face no serious challenges until autumn 1988.

Meanwhile Des Traynor had left Guinness & Mahon in 1986 and become chairman of CRH, one of the most wealthy and influential companies in the State. He was operating from an office in Fitzwilliam

Square and continued to organise the deposits for the bank in the
Caymans. When its new Japanese owners bought the parent company in
London, they had an audit done on the books of Guinness & Mahon in
Dublin and the Cayman bank, now called Ansbacher Cayman. The
Japanese were very concerned because of 'a high risk of mismanagement
or fraud' and, they discovered, 'no attempt is made to obtain third party
confirmation of balances or customer accounts.' Traynor had bought the
loan from AIB. He held it in Guinness & Mahon and moved it to
Ansbacher Cayman. The new Japanese owners didn't care if Haughey
was a Prime Minister: they wanted the loan sorted out. Traynor had to
move fast.

In November 1987, Des Traynor wrote out a list of half a dozen
wealthy businessmen who he thought may put up £150,000 to pay off
Haughey's debt. He rang Noel Fox, the auditor of Dunnes Stores and a
trustee who had the confidence of Ben Dunne. He told Fox that Haughey
had a 'significant' problem and explained his plan to put a consortium
together to bail out the Taoiseach. Noel Fox, who had the adjoining locker
to Dunne at Portmarnock Golf Club, said he would speak to Ben. He did
so after the eight o'clock management meeting they had at Dunnes
headquarters each weekday morning and stressed the confidential nature
of the request.

Ben Dunne said, 'I think Haughey is making a huge mistake trying to
get six or seven people together ... Christ picked twelve apostles and one
of them crucified him.' Dunne agreed to pay all the money, which he
thought was around £700,000, although he added that he would not be
able to pay it until the middle of 1988 and because of the sensitivity and
confidentiality of the arrangement, he said it would be sourced from
abroad.

But Traynor needed the money urgently. He called Fox again a few
days later and the accountant spoke to Ben Dunne who immediately
instructed Fox to contact the manager of the Dunnes Stores branch in
Bangor, Co. Down and draw a sterling cheque equivalent to £205,000,
payable to a John Furze. A sterling cheque for £182,630 was sent in the
post to Fox that evening, and he passed it on to Traynor.

On 8 December, Traynor sent the cheque to Guinness & Mahon in
London and asked them to credit it to the account of Ansbacher Cayman,
and when the funds were cleared to send the money on to Ansbacher
Cayman's account in Guinness & Mahon Dublin. But Traynor then rang
and changed the arrangements, and the net result was that Ben Dunne's
£205,000 was used to pay off Haughey's £105,000 debt to the Agricultural

Credit Corporation, and £59,000 was withdrawn in cash for Mr Haughey. The balance of £40,000 was then paid into the account from which Haughey Boland paid off Charles Haughey's personal and household bills.

Haughey continued to gain the admiration and respect of many of his most vocal critics through 1988 and in July, Fox received another of the 'Noel, we have a problem' calls from Des Traynor. This time it was bigger and the funds had to be paid into an account at Barclays Bank in Knightsbridge, London in the name of 'J. Furze'. Ben Dunne arranged for £471,000 sterling to be paid through a firm of Swiss lawyers to Credit Suisse in Zurich and transferred to the J. Furze account in London. The money was then moved to Guinness Mahon in London and finished up in the Ansbacher Cayman deposit account back in Guinness & Mahon in Dublin.

Haughey became seriously ill in the summer of 1988, and reports at the time said he nearly died and had been revived in the hospital after a routine procedure for kidney stones went wrong. However his economic strategy was exceeding the most optimistic forecasts and a tax amnesty, expected to raise £30 million, provided another £500 million. The downside was that rumours of collusion between Haughey and the country's biggest beef processor and exporter, Larry Goodman were whispered around the Dáil.

In April 1989, a 'Noel, we have another problem' call from Des Traynor raised a further £150,000 sterling from Ben Dunne for Haughey via a convoluted money trail, this time though the Royal Bank of Scotland and ultimately finding its way to the Ansbacher Cayman account in Guinness & Mahon in Dublin.

Upon returning home, extremely grumpy, from a trip to Japan, Haughey embarked on a series of ego-driven impulse decisions which ultimately led to a general election on 15 June and his party dropping four seats. Haughey was forced to bring Fianna Fáil into a coalition government for the first time, and it was a partnership with the Progressive Democrats led by his old enemy, Des O'Malley.

That summer, Haughey visited Australia where he formed a close friendship with the Australian Prime Minister, Bob Hawke. The year before, a close associate of Hawke's, Brian Burke, had been posted to Dublin as Australian ambassador and became a close friend of Haughey. In February 1989, Burke was loaned £10,000 by Traynor and a further £69,000 in November. Two years later, he was loaned another £91,000. In all, Burke admitted receiving nine loans totalling about £200,000 over the two years. However, Traynor claimed he gave Burke only £129,000 and that he had repaid almost £80,000. In 1994 Burke was jailed on corruption charges arising from his period as premier of Western Australia. Whether or not Haughey agreed that Burke's loans should be given by Traynor from the money provided by Ben Dunne never emerged.

Haughey strutted Napoleonically around Europe during Ireland's EU Presidency in the first six months of 1990. Later that year, Alan Dukes was replaced by John Bruton as leader of Fine Gael. Dick Spring insisted that there should be an election for the Presidency of Ireland when it came up in November. There hadn't been a Presidential election since 1973 and Spring persuaded Mary Robinson to stand for Labour.

In February 1990, Traynor made another call to Noel Fox at Dunnes Stores. This time, Des Traynor said Haughey needed £200,000 sterling and gave instructions for it to be paid into Ansbacher Cayman's account at Henry Ansbacher & Company in London, from where it was ultimately transferred to Ansbacher Cayman's account with Guinness & Mahon in Dublin. But the angel of debt at Dunnes Stores, Noel Fox, had not been forgotten. He had been put on the Customs House Docks Development Authority in 1987 and appointed as a full-time director of Voluntary Health Insurance in 1988. In 1991 he joined the board of Aer Rianta and was reappointed in 1996 by Michael Lowry – he was also auditor of Lowry's company Streamline.

There was often a queue of major figures from the world of business and finance waiting to see Haughey at Abbeville on Saturday mornings. But no matter how wealthy, powerful, influential or even generous they were, there was no doubt who was boss. Haughey liked the material benefits commerce brought to his door but he believed most successful business types were shallow and ill-educated, with a narrow range of interests and incapable of seeing the big picture. By 1990, he believed in his own ability to run the country and provide a healthy economy where the businessmen could prosper. But they should also be grateful and pay their dues – a sort of tithe. Ideally, they should also pay them off-shore, into anonymous numbered accounts, away from nosey parkers and prying eyes ....

Chapter Seven

As a man who believes golf is a metaphor for life, Ben Dunne would have seen Michael Lowry more as a useful caddie than the captain's prize. Although the TD for Tipperary North may have flattered himself and impressed his cronies by claiming him as a friend, Dunne would have filed Lowry under the heading 'supplier of services'.

In 1988, Dunnes Stores already had 90 outlets and had plans to open more. And while he was officially listed as 'joint managing director' with his brother Frank since their father's death in 1983, in reality, Ben Dunne had total control of the financial affairs of the company. He took his responsibility for expanding the business and developing new stores as an inherited imperative. Lest they forget, a photograph of Ben Dunne Senior was prominently displayed in the staff rooms of every store. Ben Dunne Junior needed no reminders of one of his father's many nuggets of homespun philosophy: 'There's no such thing as getting to the top. There's no top. When you get to the top you go down the other side.'

Dunnes Stores were Ireland's biggest retailers and traded across continents and time zones, yet Ben Dunne still paid a lot of attention to the minutiae of the business. It was only a matter of time before he homed in on the increasing importance of refrigeration and its escalating cost to the company.

In the late 1980s, when Dunnes were opening new stores all over Ireland and England, one of the biggest costs of fitting out new stores was installing refrigeration and then maintaining it. Apart from the aisles of refrigerated display units, each premises needed deep freezes and cold rooms to store fresh and frozen produce. Working on tight profit margins, a breakdown or wrong temperature setting in the refrigeration or cold rooms could spoil produce and cost money. Ben Dunne needed an expert to take care of the cold chain as it was known, someone who would do whatever he wanted, whenever he needed it done: a specialist prepared to trade their expertise for cash.

He saw himself as a shrewd talent scout, and while young Lowry was somewhat inarticulate and unsophisticated, Ben Dunne was rather uncouth himself. Maybe, like many powerful men, Ben Dunne saw something of himself in his prodigy's raw hunger for success. He had plans for Michael Lowry. It is unlikely Ben Dunne told him that his ultimate plan was to make the recently elected TD a wholly-owned human subsidiary of Dunnes Stores. Just as Michael Lowry would hardly have raised principled objections to sublimating control of his company to Ben Dunne. And Lowry wouldn't be unique: anyone, or any company, who signed on as a supplier ran the risk of becoming subsumed into the mother company.

In his rush to be rich and famous, feared and powerful, Michael Lowry must have looked an easy mark. Everything and everybody has a price in Ben's world, and in November 1988 Michael Lowry and his scruples were on Ben Dunne's Christmas shopping list. Elected to the Dáil in 1987 and appointed Fine Gael's junior spokesman on industry and commerce just a month before, Michael Lowry must have believed the last of his three wishes was within his grasp when he was told Ben wanted to see him. He was still driving a car supplied by Butler Refrigeration and being paid commission on sales by the company in Thurles, but that was part of a past which he was determined to leave behind.

Owen Molloy was the go-between. He had started as a store manager with Dunnes Stores and was appointed area manager for Munster where he first met, and became friendly with, Michael Lowry. A GAA enthusiast, he shared an interest in sport with Lowry whom he saw in work nearly every day. When Owen Molloy was appointed operations manager for Northern Ireland and the United Kingdom, Butler Refrigeration was designing and installing the refrigeration equipment at their store in Billingham. He contacted his old friend, Michael Lowry, and asked him to design the refrigeration layouts for planned Dunnes stores in the United Kingdom and Northern Ireland.

Lowry was to design the layout and specify the technical requirements, advertise for contractors and oversee the commissioning of the contract, then ensure there was an ongoing maintenance system for the new stores. Dunnes Stores' annual refrigeration maintenance costs could be cut by 30 per cent and he would install new equipment on a cost-only basis, saving the company the suppliers' normal mark up.

He was at the opening of a new store in Bradford with Owen Molloy in November 1988 when Ben Dunne asked him what he was doing there. Then Dunne turned to Owen Molloy and pointedly said he didn't want Butlers involved in the United Kingdom. He asked Lowry to contact him at his office in Dublin. It was January 1989 before they met and Ben

Dunne said he was taking the contract for supplying and servicing the refrigeration at Dunnes Stores away from Butler Refrigeration and offered Lowry the first option.

According to both Lowry and Dunne, the decision for Lowry to set up his own refrigeration servicing company only arose at the January meeting. In fact, Lowry had quietly incorporated his company, Garuda, trading under the name Streamline Enterprises, four months before this meeting, on 11 August 1988.

Matt Butler also finds it hard to reconcile Lowry and Dunne's version of events with the memory of how his business was decimated. Butlers had built up a good relationship with Dunnes over the previous ten years, doing a substantial amount of the design and layout of refrigeration units as well as servicing equipment.

In January 1989, Matt Butler was on a family skiing holiday when his secretary rang from the office in Thurles and told him Michael Lowry was leaving the company, taking key members of staff and the contract for Dunnes Stores with him. Lowry avoided the office and returned the company's Nissan Bluebird directly to the garage without saying goodbye to any of his former colleagues. It was a bitter parting; Matt Butler and Michael Lowry haven't spoken since. After losing the Dunnes contract in 1989, Butler's workforce steadily dropped from 41 to four; the same number employed in 1971, the year Lowry joined as an apprentice.

A few days after his initial meeting, Michael Lowry attended another meeting with Dunne who told him bluntly that the only reason he was setting Lowry up in business was to save money for the company. Any notions of being his own man, or of holding out for his independence, must have vanished when Dunne called in Michael Irwin, the Chief Accountant: Lowry left the office with a deal to supply and install refrigeration in the 16 Dunnes Stores in Munster. A few weeks later, Lowry's company, Streamline, had its contract extended to cover the entire Republic of Ireland. Lowry's arrangement with Dunnes was brutally simple: he was to be, in effect, a wholly-owned subsidiary, although he could, and did, masquerade to others as an independent contractor. But Streamline would exist for only one purpose: to service Dunnes Stores.

Michael Irwin, Chief Accountant at Dunnes Stores was to have, at 24 hours notice, full access to Streamline's books and records. Dunnes Stores' auditors, Oliver Freaney & Company, were also appointed auditors of the new company. Streamline was now, in reality, a division of Dunnes Stores.

When they determined the final terms of his contract, Lowry was told his company would be allowed to make a small annual profit which Michael Irwin suggested would be between £20,000 and £50,000. The chief accountant went on to say that Lowry would be paid bonuses separately by Ben Dunne, who would decide how much and how often at his own discretion. Ben Dunne told Lowry, '... if you are good for Dunnes Stores and if you achieve the savings that I think are possible, I will certainly make it worth your while and your company will be successful and you will be a wealthy man.' But it didn't come cheap. The ambitious young TD for Tipperary North's political fate and his financial future was now in the gift of the country's wealthiest and most successful businessman.

Lowry wrote to Michael Irwin, the chief accountant at Dunnes Stores, referring to his discussion with Ben Dunne, and setting out the arrangements and costs of providing the services to be undertaken by Streamline. He listed wages, transport, motor and van expenses, insurance, lease of office and store, light and heat, even to the detail of telephone charges, stationary and postage charges. There were labour charges for five men doing 40 hours per week for 49 weeks. Motor and van expenses came to £21,006. Expenses were divided by the number of hours, 9,800, working out at a rate of £14.14 per hour. This all came to a total of £138,622.

A company owned by Lowry and his wife, Green Holdings, was to own the headquarters at Abbey Road, Thurles, where they would build a warehouse and office, at a cost of some £57,000. However the land actually became the property of Garuda, the holding company of Streamline. Dunne agreed to give Streamline a free loan and it was to be repaid by allowing Streamline to create an 'imaginary profit' of around £50,000 a year for four years. In both Dunnes Stores' and Streamline's books these payments were treated as a loan. But it was an exercise in cosmetic bookeeping. It was really an internal matter, as if one division of Dunnes Stores paid another £165,000. This transaction was recorded as a legitimate loan in the books of both Streamline and Dunnes Stores which were certified by Oliver Freaney & Company, the auditors of the two companies.

Lowry's arrangement with Dunnes Stores was a dark secret, although the perception of Lowry and Streamline as one of the country's biggest refrigeration contractors added to his growing reputation as a successful businessman. He was turning heads in Tipperary, upgrading his car and discovering bespoke tailoring. Using his elevated status as a shrewd deal-maker to raise his profile in in Fine Gael, he sniffed the wind and distanced himself from the leader, Alan Dukes. The rich mix of politics and business allowed Lowry an entrée into an altogether more sophisticated society. Some of his colleagues in Fine Gael mistook his silences for stupidity, but that was mistaken. He was taciturn and he was unsure of himself socially. But he seemed to know about money. His reputation as a fund-raiser for the GAA spread beyond Tipperary after the success of Féile in Thurles.

Thurles takes its responsibilities as the birthplace of the GAA very seriously and ran up debts of some £1.2 million preparing Semple Stadium for the centenary celebrations in 1984. The year before, the fund-raising committee had come up with a double-your-money scheme. It was very ambitious and, even if it took ten years, guaranteed doubling the amount of money paid in by subscribers. Some companies which contributed eventually wrote off their subscriptions. But the committee was faced with the continuing headache of repaying their investors. The chairman, Father Pierce Duggan, left the committee and the priesthood, and Michael Lowry, who had just stepped down as the youngest ever chairman of the county board, took over in 1987.

MCD, a concert promotions company in Dublin, had been trying to persuade the Semple Stadium fund-raising committee to run a rock festival in Thurles since 1986. When Michael Lowry took over he was in favour but Noel Morris, the county chairman who replaced him, was opposed to a festival and in 1989 came up with the idea of a clubs' draw which eventually cleared over half Semple Stadium's £1.2m debt. Michael Lowry, the go-ahead young TD, identified himself very publicly with the rock festival and eventually coaxed and cajoled a majority of the committee to vote in favour. Denis Desmond of MCD said the GAA was on a percentage of the profits, with a guarantee of some £30,000 up to £70,000.

The festival was called Féile '90, it caught the imagination of young people all over Ireland and some 70,000 arrived in Thurles for that August bank holiday weekend. As well as their cash contribution, MCD was also obliged to provide facilities such as toilets in the stadium. Van Morrison, Christy Moore, Mary Black, An Emotional Fish, Hothouse Flowers and supporting acts played to rapturous audiences. A Garda spokesman said it had been an exceptionally quiet considering the size of the crowds, although some fans suffered minor burns caused by phosphorous spilling from luminous headbands.

A spokesman for the promoters told *The Irish Times* the total cost of the event was £600,000 including £40,000 paid to the GAA, which would also get an undisclosed percentage of the profits. Some 20,000 young people

each paid just under £30 a ticket. Seven years later, sources said their
books show the GAA was paid £79,553 by MCD in 1990. Lowry promoted
MCD's cause at meetings the committee held in Hayes Hotel in Thurles
and took a very public stance in favour of Féile both in Tipperary and
nationally. The next year the Trip to Tipp meant a three mile tail-back of
traffic and over-stuffed trains headed for Thurles over the August
weekend. Elvis Costello, the Pogues, Nancy Griffith, Van Morrison, a
total of 27 acts over three days, attracted 120,000 to a town already
overstretched coping with 50,000 for the Munster Hurling Final. The
GAA was paid £149,760 by MCD in 1991.

By 1992, locals were beginning to weary of the invasion but Michael
Lowry stoutly defended it and the GAA nearly doubled its money on the
previous year. Costs were escalating for MCD but the American group
Talking Heads attracted another enormous crowd and the GAA's books
show they made £147,324. Michael Lowry bought a fine new period
house in Holycross which locals nicknamed, Teach Féile. Rumours swept
around Thurles that Lowry was on a cut of the profits, but Denis
Desmond said he had smoothed over local irritation by chairing meetings
and giving away free tickets. 'He was paid nothing in fees', according to
Desmond. 'All the money went to the GAA. We wondered why he was
doing it. He did it for Thurles ... for the votes.'

Desmond claims 1993 was a disaster. 'We lost substantial money on
Chris de Burgh. We made a mistake and lost £500,000. Chris de Burgh's
audience were not into standing in a field.' It was also the year that de
Burgh caused a controversy by hiring a stripper to appear on stage with
him. At the end of the weekend, MCD paid the GAA £81,487, however
the promoters still owed them £57,000. Lowry used the debt to tell the
committee that if the 1994 Féile didn't go ahead, they would never get the
money from MCD. Between the draw and the Féile, which had
contributed a total of £515,524, if the £57,000 owed by MCD is included,
the debt of more than £1 million on Semple Stadium was nearly cleared.

However, opposition from the local Archbishop, traders and the
townspeople of Thurles was growing. The last Trip to Tipp, which MCD
said was mainly staged to clear the £57,000 debt to the GAA, featured
Crowded House, Björk, Blur and Elvis Costello. But the most memorable
exercise at the final Féile in Thurles was the excessive drinking which
began on the Friday night and continued until Monday morning.

After failing to get into government following the election in 1989,
when Fianna Fáil made an historic coalition with the Progressive
Democrats, Fine Gael continued to languish in the opinion polls. Alan

Dukes' leadership was coming under increasing pressure in 1990 and the upcoming presidential election was becoming a focus for discontent in the parliamentary party. In response to the criticism of his leadership, Dukes promised he would produce 'a strong and electable' candidate.

The parliamentary party prepared itself for the inevitable heave and Michael Lowry ingratiated himself with John Bruton, although he made sure to stay friendly with Bruton's potential rivals for the leadership, Michael Noonan and Ivan Yates. John Bruton's elevation to the leadership in late 1990 failed to halt the decline in the public's support for Fine Gael through 1991. Lowry spent much of his time in opposition in the early 1990s developing his refrigeration business with Dunnes Stores, although he didn't neglect his constituency. In the general election held in November 1992, the Fine Gael vote in Tipperary North dropped by less than two per cent although nationally the party had its worst showing for 45 years and dropped ten seats. And, more ominously, there were murmurings of dissatisfaction about the leadership, with Michael Noonan and Ivan Yates rumoured to be potential challengers.

His rivals acknowledged that Michael Lowry was an extremely well-organised politician who ran his election machine with military precision. Others thought the enormous amount of time and attention he gave to what were apparently inconsequential constituency matters indicated an inherent vulnerability. But if insecurity is an occupational condition for elected politicians who regularly have to seek the approval of a fickle public, it is also a powerful motivator for a businessman desperately seeking success.

In the early 1990s, the former apprentice refrigeration engineer from Holycross could have written a paper on productive time management for the Harvard Business School. Where did he find the time to babysit the electorate of Tipperary North while furthering his ambitions for national politics? Why did he insist on remaining a kingpin in the dog-eat-dog world of GAA politics? How could he afford the energy to become a key organiser for the country's premier rock festival? All of this and run Streamline, his successful and continually expanding refrigeration service company.

To the rest of the world, Michael Lowry was his own man, even something of a superman, and Streamline, his company, the source of his considerable affluence. Anyone sufficiently interested to enquire, would have discovered that Dunnes Stores was a major customer, but few would have guessed it was his only customer. He was saving them a lot of money, and, by allowing Lowry to keep up the pretence that he was an independent contractor, Dunnes Stores saved his face.

Dunnes Stores had covered the start-up costs for Lowry's company and they paid the agreed invoices for routine work done by Streamline. But Ben Dunne had told Michael Lowry he would make him a wealthy man and neither of them allowed the law, or tax considerations, to get in the way. Incredibly, Ben Dunne hadn't specified exactly how Lowry would achieve his wealth, and Michael Lowry was anxious not to offend his benefactor by asking awkward questions. There had been talk of bonuses, but all Lowry knew was that Ben had given him his word and to a man's man like Ben Dunne, his word was his bond.

Most of the cheques paid to Lowry on Ben Dunne's instructions were drawn on a Dunnes Stores account in a branch of the Bank of Ireland in Marino, Dublin, an account which, astonishingly, none of the other directors knew about. It was an indication of Ben Dunne's total control over the company's finances at that time. There were five cheques made payable to Lowry personally: one for £6,000 drawn on 20 December 1989 which he cashed; another for £8,500 on 21 December 1990 which he paid into his personal account of the Bank of Ireland in Thurles; a cheque for £6,500 dated 10 July 1991 which he paid into his personal account in the Dame Street branch of the Allied Irish Bank in Dublin; another for £8,000 dated 11 December 1991 payable to cash and again lodged in the personal account in the AIB on Dame Street, Dublin; a cheque for £12,000, dated 15 December 1992, also payable to cash, which Lowry cashed. Later, it would be claimed that five of these cheques were to pay bonuses to the staff at Streamline, and the £6,500 cheque was to settle an expenses claim by Lowry.

However some of the the payments Dunnes Stores made to Streamline were even more questionable. Between November 1988 and March 1993, Lowry either cashed, or lodged to his own account, nine cheques issued by Dunnes for Streamline, for a total value of nearly £160,000. The first, and the only one in Irish currency, was for £6,000 drawn on 14 November 1988 and lodged to Lowry's personal account in the Bank of Ireland in Thurles, County Tipperary. The next six, issued between 13 December 1988 and 14 September 1990, were all in sterling and varied between £5,000 and £19,730.

The most intriguing transaction concerns a payment of £34,100 sterling, which was part of a £100,000 lodgement Lowry used to open an off-shore account in Allied Irish Banks in Jersey on 3 September 1991. Lowry had another two off-shore accounts in the Isle of Man which were opened for him on the instructions of Ben Dunne but the secret off-shore account in Jersey was entirely his own idea. No one else, neither Ben Dunne nor anyone in Dunne Stores, knew about it. The Channel Islands account was held in the name of Lowry and his three children and, presumably, it was to be his financial security blanket, a nest egg hidden away for emergencies or his old age. There is no explanation of where he obtained the balance of £65,900 to make up the £100,000 lodgement on 3 September 1991.

Another payment of £55,314 sterling was lodged by Lowry into his personal account held at the Allied Irish Banks branch on Dame Street Dublin on 15 March 1993. Lowry maintained that this was money paid to him for work he did personally as a consultant, but records in Dunnes Stores show that Streamline invoiced them for exactly same amount and it was for work done by the company. Neither Ben Dunne nor Michael Irwin, the accountant who negotiated his financial arrangements with the company, said Lowry was ever retained as a consultant on a personal basis. The evidence suggests that Michael Lowry took the money from the company for his own benefit.

The bonuses paid to Lowry by Dunnes Stores also present him with another problem, The first £25,000 bonus was paid in three sterling cheques drawn on 9 October 1990 from Dunnes Stores' account in the Bank of Ireland at Marino, Dublin. Lowry lodged the cheques to an account held in his own name at the Bank of Ireland in the Isle of Man, which Ben Dunne suggested he open. Lowry transferred the monies to an account he held in the Irish Permanent Building Society in Cork on 20 May 1992. On 1 August 1991, Ben Dunne had £40,000 sterling transferred from Tutbury Limited, an Isle of Man company he controlled, to Rea Brothers, an Isle of Man bank where the money was lodged to an account in the name of Badgeworth Limited.

Dunne had instructed his solicitor to incorporate a company for Lowry on the Isle of Man and open an account at Rea Brothers bank in the company's name. Lowry said he didn't know he was the owner of Badgeworth Limited or that the company had an account in Rea Brothers Bank. However, on 18 May 1992 he closed the Badgeworth account and transferred the money, which, with interest, was now £42,567.26 sterling, to an account he held in the Irish Permanent Building Society in Cork.

Lowry endorsed the back of a cheque for £50,000 payable to Streamline Enterprises, drawn from a Dunnes Stores account in the Ulster Bank on College Green, Dublin, and paid it into his account at the Irish Permanent

Building Society in Cork. On 29 May 1992, a bank draft drawn on the Bank of Ireland on the instructions of Rea brothers Bank in the Isle of Man, was paid into Lowry's account at the Irish Permanent Building Society in Cork.

Mr Lowry needed a lot of money in 1992. Besides the £90,000 he collected from Dunnes Stores in two days at the end of May, he also had £100,000 on deposit in the Channel Islands. He had his eye on a property in Holycross, one of the finest Georgian houses in the county, Glenreigh House, which had been a Church of Ireland rectory until 1937. Set in 32 acres, it was a handsome three-bay, two-storey house with a magnificent hallway and staircase, which was owned by an elderly woman living alone, Ms Diane Turner. The Lowry family lived in a bungalow nearby and had the luxury of being able to purchase the new house, which needed extensive refurbishment, without selling their current residence.

Lowry rang Ben Dunne and told him he needed money for the rebuilding and extension of the house, then spoke to Dunnes Stores' accountant, Michael Irwin and asked him to recommend an architect and a builder. Lowry bought the house for £140,000, less than a week before the public auction. And because he had considerably more than the purchase price in his deposit account at the Irish Permanent Building Society in Cork, he was allowed to borrow £140,000, the full price of the house.

Ben Dunne thought £200,000 would cover the building work, but, like his promises of bonuses, nothing specific was agreed with Lowry. Michael Irwin told Lowry that a Dublin-based architect, Peter Stevens, and a building contractor in Co. Kildare, Faxhill Homes, worked for Dunnes Stores and had built extensively on Ben Dunne's house, and he suggested Lowry tell them to do the work. Both the architect and the builder contacted Ben Dunne to get the go ahead.

Peter Stevens had the job costed by a quantity surveyor who gave a preliminary price of £216,000. By the time the house was completed however, it cost nearly twice the estimate and Dunnes Stores paid the builders £395,000 for the refurbishment and extension to Lowry's house.

Michael Irwin asked Ben Dunne how the builder's and architect's bills should be paid. The accountant argued that the method Ben Dunne had in mind was a bad deal for the company, that if the cost was treated as a payment to Streamline or Michael Lowry, it would be tax deductible for Dunnes Stores. Ben's decision prevailed: in the company's books, the £395,000 was recorded as work done at the Dunnes Stores branch in the Ilac Centre in Dublin.

In theory, selling Fine Gael was not very different from flogging refrigerators and Michael Lowry's experienced foot-in-the-door technique unlocked a lot of cash for his party. In politics, business, sport, religion, even charities, goodwill is a convertible currency and giving obliges the receiver to at least think kindly of the donor. This ethically-sensitive truism was not lost on Michael Lowry. His fund-raising for the GAA in Tipperary had reaped him a huge political bonus, and he realised that if he put the trustees of Fine Gael in his debt, it would have huge potential for his future.

It is hard to pinpoint exactly when Lowry realised that his lucrative business relationship with Ben Dunne could also profit his political career. But his own experience, and the legendary stories of Dunne's apparently limitless largesse, must have fired his imagination. His personal benefactor, Ben Dunne, gave his leader, Alan Dukes, £30,000 after a dinner at Barberstown Castle, Co. Kildare, with a promise of more, in October 1989, but that meeting was arranged by a Galwayman, John Mulholland. Alan Dukes' popularity in and outside the party continued to slip through 1990, and Lowry quietly switched his personal allegiance to John Bruton, who was already being openly spoken about as the future leader of Fine Gael.

While his contributions to the Dáil were rare, his fund-raising activities for the GAA, particularly the Féile weekends in Thurles, were the talk of the country. In November 1990, when John Bruton was elected leader of the party, Fine Gael was deeply in debt with annual running costs of several hundred thousand pounds. It was languishing in the opinion polls, with little prospect of attaining office, which, in turn, made fund-raising even more difficult. By definition, most political leaders are vain and find fund-raising distasteful, even demeaning, believing their talents are for shaping the future of the nation. They feel cheapened by glad-handing, shaking down and writing begging letters to potential donors. That's why natural salesmen like Michael Lowry, who suffer no embarrassment or see no loss of dignity in soliciting cash for their cause, are so useful to, and quietly valued by, political parties.

Early in 1991 Fine Gael debts had reached £1.3 million, throwing the party into a financial crisis, and John Bruton was grateful when Lowry offered to help. Bruton later said he didn't know Ben Dunne had already contributed £30,000 to Alan Dukes in October 1989, when Michael Lowry suggested to him that they would approach Dunne for a donation to Fine Gael in 1991. It was Lowry who arranged for Bruton to call at Ben Dunne's home in Castleknock, halfway between his home in Co. Meath and the Dáil. Bruton called on the evening of 24 April 1991. Michael

Lowry was already in the house when Ben Dunne and his wife, Mary, opened the door and each of them greeted Bruton with a handshake. Lowry had already made it clear to Dunne that the purpose of the meeting was for a donation to Fine Gael, so there was no need for Bruton to raise the embarrassing subject of money when the three men went into a quiet room.

Bruton admired the house and its grounds, they talked generally about politics, then moved on to other small talk. Lowry excused himself, leaving Bruton and Dunne in the room together. Tea was served, the conversation continued for nearly an hour before Ben Dunne gave John Bruton a Dunnes Stores cheque for £50,000. It was drawn on the same branch of the Bank of Ireland at Marino, Dublin, as he had used to pay other monies to Michael Lowry. It wasn't the first time Ben Dunne had given money to Bruton. In 1988 he had given Fine Gael TD Jim Mitchell a cheque for £5,000 after meeting him casually in a local pub and told him to share it with Bruton.

Fine Gael was ill-prepared for the 1992 general election, even though the coalition government of Fianna Fáil and the Progressive Democrats had been under strain for months. John Bruton had not made an impact as leader and the party continued to slump in the opinion polls. A group of backbenchers had seen Michael Noonan as a possible alternative leader and while Lowry had publicly endorsed John Bruton, he decided to base his quiet friendship with Noonan on a more material foundation. In 1991 Noonan was formally introduced to Dunne in his office at Dunnes Stores headquarters in Dublin by Michael Lowry. The next time was in 1992, just after the November election, when he visited Ben Dunne in hospital at the invitation of Michael Lowry.

During the election campaign, Lowry invited Noonan to speak at a rally in his Tipperary North constituency. Lowry told Noonan he had a contribution from Ben Dunne and handed him a cheque for £3,000. A year later, Dunne gave Noonan £2,000 and a year after that, in 1994, another cheque for £1,000; both contributions were for his Limerick East constituency funds. Another leadership contender in Fine Gael, Ivan Yates, was phoned by Lowry during the 1992 general election. Lowry told Yates he had received £5,000 for his personal campaign funds from Ben Dunne. Yates had never met Dunne but his contribution was ten times bigger than the previous largest donation ever made to him.

The Wexford TD's sister drove to Dublin and collected the sealed envelope containing £5,000 in cash from a receptionist at a city centre hotel. A few weeks after the election, Lowry arranged for Ivan Yates to thank his benefactor at a meeting in the Conrad Hotel in Dublin. The three of them met in the bar and talked for almost an hour. Ben Dunne did most of the talking: he spoke about his father, the money his wife's boutique was losing and his difficulties after the scandal in Orlando earlier that year. Ivan Yates found Ben Dunne fascinating: it was the first time he had ever seen anyone drinking pints of Heineken 'with loads of ice in it'.

In the wake of a disastrous election where the party had its worst results for almost 45 years and lost ten seats, the crisis within Fine Gael deepened when they again failed to enter government. John Bruton's endorsement as leader three weeks before hadn't removed the threat to his position and an air of gloom hung over the parliamentary party when they met on 9 February 1993. The first business of the post-election what-went-wrong meeting was to elect a new party chairman. Three weeks previously, the parliamentary party had reaffirmed John Bruton's leadership and faced into the twenty-seventh Dáil with debts of nearly £1 million. Ben Dunne's discreet largesse-by-proxy to the party, and its most senior figures, at the discretion of Michael Lowry, would not emerge for another five years.

It was expected to be a tight contest between two senior party figures, Bernard Allen, the front bench spokesman on social welfare, and John Browne who had been acting chairman. Michael Lowry, an unknown quantity to many backbenchers, only declared himself a contender less than a week before the meeting at the urging of Ivan Yates. Traditionally, the chairman is a long-serving member who can act as a father figure, and most observers and backbenchers were taken aback when Lowry was declared the winner after taking over half the votes, 30 out of a total of 58. The ubiquitous senior party sources said the election of Lowry was 'a clear signal that the party wants action. We need to decentralise the party; we need to reform and change and Michael Lowry is viewed as young and capable of representing change.'

The party's huge debts were still a major worry to the Micawber tendency in the Fine Gael hierarchy, and rather than give Lowry a front bench portfolio, Bruton appointed his party chairman Director of Party Finances a month later. It was a measure of Bruton's trust in Lowry and the desperation of the party's financial plight. Lowry went about his task with relish. In early September 1993, after further attacks on Bruton's leadership, Lowry said Fine Gael's debt had been reduced from more than £1.2m to £900,000. He added that the debt target of £500,000 for 1993 could still be met. He clearly knew something to which few in his party were privy: a very secret £100,000 donation from Ben Dunne.

As chairman of the party trustees, Lowry spoke to the party's general secretary, Ivan Doherty, in May and told him Ben Dunne had delivered a cheque for £100,000. He emphasised that Dunne wished for his donation to be kept confidential. The £100,000 cheque, made payable to cash, was sent to Ivan Doherty in the internal post. Anxious to preserve Dunne's confidentiality, Doherty lodged the cheque in a dormant account he held in the name of 'I. Doherty trading as Public Relations and Research Enterprise' and then immediately wrote out and lodged a cheque for £100,000 from that account, payable to Fine Gael.

It had been a memorable year in Lowry's long march from the relative obscurity of the backbenches to the inner sanctum of Fine Gael. This was the year he had purchased the grandest house in his home village of Holycross and become a local hero for halving the GAA's million-pound debt. 1993 saw Michael Lowry establish his reputation nationally and secure his position as a senior and trusted member of John Bruton's inner group of advisers. Ben Dunne's money had bought Michael Lowry a lot of influence at the highest levels of Fine Gael.

The collapse of the Fianna Fáil-Labour government in November 1994 was a consequence of deep personal enmity between Taoiseach Albert Reynolds and Tanaiste Dick Spring. They had clashed over the fallout from the beef tribunal report, the appointment of a President of the High Court and the failure of the Attorney General's office to extradite a paedophile priest, Father Brendan Smyth, to Northern Ireland. After Albert Reynolds resigned as Taoiseach, rather than dissolve the Dáil and seek an election from the President, senior politicians began a tortuous round of negotiations to come up with another combination of parties to form a government.

John Bruton asked his brother Richard, a TD for 12 years and one of the most respected and best-liked members in the Dáil, and Michael Lowry, described at the time as 'one of John Bruton's most trusted confidants' to negotiate for Fine Gael. Lowry had no illusions: he told friends that if Fine Gael didn't get into government, the party didn't have a future. Pointedly, he refused to rule out the notion of Dick Spring sharing the role of Taoiseach with John Bruton. In the negotiations, their desperation obvious: Fine Gael conceded nearly every demand made of them by Labour and Democratic Left. It was Michael Lowry who said yes to a seat at the cabinet table for Democratic Left's Pat Rabbitte, the final detail of the agreement for the Rainbow Coalition, in the chamber of the Dáil, just before John Bruton was elected Taoiseach.

Chapter Eight

Charles Haughey was Taoiseach when he became eligible for the free travel scheme he introduced for pensioners 24 years earlier. Although he had reached the age qualification for a pensioner in September 1990, many of his attitudes were closer to a new lad's than an old codger's. His role model was a septuagenarian, François Mitterrand, who had already been his house guest on Inishvickillane when they met at the EC summit in Dublin in June 1990. A lifelong Francophile, Haughey spent holidays on the Riviera and loftily declared to his friends that civilisation ends at the northern shores of the Mediterranean. Paris was his favourite city. He had spent memorable romantic weekends at the Raphael or Meurice Hotels, and when he visited Paris officially as Taoiseach, a dozen motorcycle outriders cleared the way for the 70 mile-an-hour dash from the airport to his hotel. Haughey admired the French President's patriarchal embrace of his people and as Taoiseach he even added Mitterrand's walk to his arsenal of Napoleonic affectations.

He was also enjoying something of an Indian summer in his political career. Despite the inevitable hiccoughs, upsets and a hare-brained general election in 1989, he had restored confidence in the economy since taking office in 1987. Haughey's competence in government had won him a grudging respect from the sniffy professional classes of Dublin who had distrusted him through nearly 40 years in public life. His age and guile counted for more than the opposition leader's youth, enthusiasm and full head of hair. There was even affection for him: the venerable Machiavellian schemer was now seen more as a lovable old rogue. Even his most ardent enemies conceded that Haughey was intellectually brilliant and his management of government business formidably efficient.

This revisionist view of Haughey was encouraged by his press adviser, PJ Mara, who never discouraged the media from portraying his client as a latter-day Renaissance man. There was a Haughey to match any occasion: Haughey the statesman; Haughey the economic genius; Haughey the common man at ease among his own people in his Dublin constituency; Haughey the self-contained philosopher isolated on his island in the wild Atlantic; Haughey the sophisticated connoisseur of fine wines, great art and literature. And there was Haughey the legendary lover of women.

Since he entered public life there had been talk of other women in his life and rather than take umbrage, he enjoyed, even encouraged, his reputation as a ladies' man. He would stop before entering a reception or function, survey the room and invariably make his way straight to the most attractive woman. She would get his undivided attention while he oozed charm, dispensed exaggerated courtesy and flirted outrageously. For some years, he had kept company with the estranged wife of a High Court judge and she wrote about their relationship in her gossip column in the *Sunday Independent* newspaper. 'The Keane Edge' was mildly satirical, always witty, occasionally scathing, sometimes hurtful, and regularly libellous. The column was the creation of the paper's features editor, Anne Harris, who wrote and rewrote some of the copy.

Terry Keane was often blamed for stories which she did not write and told friends that the bitchy character portrayed as the author of 'The Keane Edge' bore little resemblance to her. She had been a fashion writer on a rival newspaper, the now defunct *Sunday Press*, and was wooed across the Liffey to the *Sunday Independent* by a combination of flattery and a fat pay cheque. An attractive woman with a husky voice, she was nearly 20 years younger than Haughey whom she had known since the days of the Three Musketeers when she had been close to Donogh O'Malley. Terry Keane was also an incorrigible flirt with expensive tastes which made other women, especially the wives of successful men, suspicious and jealous.

Still, she encouraged her reputation as a femme fatale. Nearly every week 'The Keane Edge' had a reference to Charles Haughey heavily laden with double entendres and written in a heavy breathing style guaranteed to raise nearly as many hackles as giggles. In the column, he was called 'Sweetie' and she gave heavy hints that her knowledge of the affairs of State was as intimate as her familiarity with his anatomy. When *The Sunday Times* wrote about Mitterrand's secret love affairs, she mused, 'Only the British would see something sinister in a prime minister having a mistress. The French know that the secret of stable government is a stable mistress .... My readers, unlike *The Sunday Times* readers, have known for many a long day about François Mitterrand's love life. He has shared many a tryst in the mist of Kerry with his *petite amie* Madame Guimaud, who has a holiday home there. And I've told you all before about the many times they entertained myself and my own *petit ami* there.

Danielle Mitterrand knows all about that too, and I doubt that she has a problem about it.'

Some of Haughey's children did have a problem with the weekly outings of their father in the *Sunday Independent*. The media was more confident in the late 1980s and early 1990s, and public figures guilty of hypocrisy found their private lives liable to be exposed. A popular weekly satirical review on RTE radio, *Scrap Saturday*, lampooned celebrities and statesmen, politicians, pop stars and business tycoons without fear or favour. Haughey's histrionic affectations were hilariously parodied by Dermot Morgan while Pauline McLynn did a wicked send up of Terry Keane's breathy pillow talk. Just a few years before, the prurient gossip about Haughey and Keane was confined to drawing-room chatter and lounge bar tittle-tattle. *Private Eye* magazine in London had chronicled their ups and downs for years, and even coined a memorable phrase to celebrate their friendship: horizontal jogging. An Irish journalist on the *Guardian* newspaper in London wrote a story about Haughey's health problems, the alleged tensions between himself and the President, and Haughey's alleged affair with the estranged wife of a High Court judge. But the mainstream Irish newspapers avoided the subject and editors argued that while it was well known to an elite circle, Mr Haughey's and Mrs Keane's private lives were their own business.

Scrap Saturday had decoded The Keane Edge's double entendres and brought the romantic notions of Sweetie and Terry onto the radio and into the homes of the *hoi polloi* every Saturday morning. One of the Haughey sons approached several friends of the writers and performers of *Scrap Saturday* and said the references to his father and Terry Keane were unfair to his mother who had been embarrassed by the scandal generated by 'The Keane Edge' and the radio programme. He was told that Charles Haughey was in the better position than anyone to stop it: all he had to do was tell Terry Keane not to write about him again.

* * *

Through the summer recess, the political parties were choosing candidates and preparing for the presidential election. Then the Dáil was recalled to pass emergency legislation to prevent the collapse of Goodman International, the Irish-based company which had become the biggest beef exporter in Europe. The company owed £460 million to a number of Irish and international banks following the Gulf War. Iraq had defaulted on payments of £180 million, but Goodman had also lost £200 million on a share-buying adventure in the British stock market. Larry Goodman had been closely associated with Haughey who had promoted his company in 1987, and he took a helicopter to Abbeville to explain his plight ten days before the Dáil was recalled on 28 August 1990.

Brian Lenihan, probably the most popular politician among his peers in Leinster House, was the Fianna Fáil presidential candidate. He wanted the nomination and, while the by-election in Dublin West could be awkward for the government if he succeeded, Haughey couldn't refuse his oldest friend. Two years before, Lenihan had undergone a successful life-saving liver transplant at the Mayo clinic in the United States. However, the long-term prognosis for patients surviving the operation was still unknown in 1989 and there were concerns about his future health.

The Fine Gael leader, Alan Dukes, had a problem. Both Garret FitzGerald and Peter Barry, the two best qualified candidates, refused to stand for the presidency, and by September, his enemies within made his handling of the presidential campaign a test of his leadership. On 5 September, Dukes told his front bench he had his candidate, a northerner and former Stormont MP, who had become a TD in Dublin West, Austin Currie. Even before his selection, market research showed his northern origins were a liability and he had a low recognition factor with voters.

Democratic Left supported Mary Robinson, the cool and detached senior counsel who had been persuaded to run earlier that year by Dick Spring and the Labour Party. The first opinion poll showed Lenihan with 53 per cent, Robinson at 32 per cent and Currie with 15 per cent. A month later, just three weeks before polling day, Lenihan had dropped to 45 per cent and Robinson had improved to 36 per cent, but Currie was only showing 19 per cent. Fine Gael knew they couldn't win, but they could do the next best thing: stop the Fianna Fáil candidate. The former leader Garret FitzGerald, and the Fine Gael Director of Elections, Jim Mitchell, came up with a plan to damage Lenihan. FitzGerald appeared on the *Questions and Answers* programme on RTÉ television to query Brian Lenihan about the events of 27 January 1982. FitzGerald claimed that senior Fianna Fáil figures had tried to ring President Hillery to prevail on him not to dissolve the Dáil. They wanted the President to request them to form a government without an election when the coalition led by FitzGerald fell. This was a discretionary power of the President under the Constitution which had never been exercised.

Lenihan said it was 'a fiction of Garret's.' FitzGerald delivered his counter-punch, '... I was in Aras an Uachtaráin when these phone calls came through and I know how many there were.' Fine Gael had another activist in the audience, Brian Murphy, and he asked Lenihan directly if he had made a phone call to the Aras that night. Lenihan said, 'No ... I want to assure you that it never happened.' Brian Murphy knew before the programme that a post-graduate student at UCD, Jim Duffy, had tape-recorded an interview with Lenihan during which he admitted phoning the President.

Four days later, Charles Haughey called Garret FitzGerald a liar in the Dáil and Bertie Ahern, Lenihan's campaign manager, said the tape recording may have been stolen from Jim Duffy. Gay Byrne challenged *The Irish Times* to put up or shut up. Although they had a copy of the tape-recording, *The Irish Times* called a press conference to highlight its existence rather than run the exclusive story in the newspaper. On the recording, Lenihan said his colleague, Sylvester Barrett, Charles Haughey and himself had all made calls to the President that night. Challenged with his own quotes on the television news, Lenihan said 'In fact, that is wrong, and I want to emphasise it here. From my mature recollection and discussion with other people, at no stage did I ring President Hillery on that occasion or at any other time.'

The junior coalition partners, the Progressive Democrats, demanded Lenihan's resignation from government. Lenihan met Haughey who told him that resigning would help his campaign and people would understand his resignation was to avoid a general election. Lenihan told his old friend that his resignation would be an admission of guilt. Queen Beatrix of the Netherlands must have wondered what was going on when she arrived for a State visit in the middle of the row. An *Irish Independent* poll found that Lenihan had fallen to just 31 per cent while Mary Robinson had soared to 51 per cent.

Alan Dukes put down a motion of 'no confidence' in the government and some of the most bitter exchanges for years echoed around the Dáil. The Labour leader, Dick Spring, said: 'This debate is not about Brian Lenihan. This debate, essentially, is about the evil spirit that controls one political party in the Republic. And it is about the way in which that spirit had begun to corrupt the entire political system in our country. This is a debate about greed, about disregard for the truth, and about contempt for political standards. It is a debate about the way in which a once great party has been brought to its knees by the grasping acquisitiveness of its leader. It is ultimately a debate about the cancer that is eating away at our body politic – and the virus which has caused that cancer, An Taoiseach Charles J. Haughey.'

Later that evening, Haughey told the Dáil, 'Brian Lenihan has been a friend, a loyal and trusted colleague with whom I have served in the Dáil for well over a quarter of a century .... Most people in the House will understand what I have to do with great sadness and great sorrow ... I propose to exercise my constitutional prerogative and advise the president to terminate his appointment as a member of the government.' Ironically, Brian Lenihan took 44.1 per cent of the vote, while Mary Robinson got 38.9 per cent. However she got nearly 77 per cent of Austin Currie's transfers and became President.

In his subsequent book, *For the Record*, Brian Lenihan explained that at the time he had given the interview, he had been on a cocktail of powerful drugs to prevent the rejection of his transplanted liver. Some academics were furious with the post-graduate student, Jim Duffy, who had broken a convention of keeping such interviews confidential. It was also another example of Fianna Fáil assuming their own guilt: there was nothing improper about contacting the President. Fine Gael, which hadn't been elected into office since 1982, went into government in December 1994 when the Fianna Fáil-Labour coalition collapsed, without the Dáil being dissolved. However, sacking Brian Lenihan did Haughey enormous damage among Fianna Fáil supporters and would ultimately destroy him.

* * *

Over the previous three years, Ben Dunne had become a regular visitor to Abbeville, but neither he nor Charles Haughey ever mentioned the money. Yet it must have hung over every conversation like cigar smoke in a nightclub. It wasn't as if Ben Dunne had slipped him a couple of grand to see him over Christmas. By February of 1990, Ben Dunne had given him more than £1 million. Haughey was a past master at leading conversations to wherever he wanted them to go, or steering them away from something awkward or unpleasant. Whatever the company, he could come up with an appropriate topic; or, if it was required, Haughey would become mute. He was using the long silence as a theatrical device when Harold Pinter was still a struggling actor. As a man who used power like a lump hammer, Ben Dunne must have been fascinated by the menace of Haughey's manipulative subtlety at their fireside chats.

No one called him Ben Junior any longer. In 1990, Dunnes Stores was the fifth largest company in the country, and in December that year they took in around £100 million, more than they had taken in over in the whole of 1980. Profits were somewhere between £55 million and £60 million and rather than borrow money, they were using their profits to expand. Ben Dunne was running the show with a group of some ten managers. He had emerged triumphant from a number of bruising confrontations since his father died six years before. The most public was at the Henry Street branch when staff went on strike rather than handle South African oranges. He insisted that if the government banned the importing of goods from the apartheid regime, he would follow suit, but meanwhile the Dunnes were in charge at Dunnes Stores. The resulting two-year strike ate into profits, but he refused to capitulate. When a bishop tried to intervene, Dunne told him, 'I see you have a gold ring on your finger. When you can prove that the gold wasn't taken from a South African mine then I'll pay heed to what you're saying.'

Ben Dunne enjoyed a good scrap and he relished his wars with British rivals and companies. A self-styled patriot, he became embroiled in a battle with a £1 billion, publicly-quoted company, British Land, which was developing the St Stephen's Green Centre in the late 1980s. Dunnes had already invested more than £12 million in the shopping complex before it was built. British Land approached one of his biggest rivals, Superquinn, and offered a lease on a 12,000 square foot site beside Dunnes Stores in the centre of the complex. Ben heard about the secret negotiations, took legal advice and told the British developer he was not opening the branch of Dunnes Stores. Without him as an anchor tenant, renting the other shops would be a problem. British Land backed down and had to give Dunnes the site promised to Superquinn at a bargain price. His reputation as a tough negotiator and bottom-line deal-maker was assured.

He still took time out to enjoy himself, working a 55-hour week and taking two family holidays each year. Four years before, the normally camera-shy retailer had become the focal point of the 1986 Irish Open when he caddied for his friend, the professional golfer, Des Smyth. He abandoned his usual dark business suit for a multi-coloured caddie's boiler suit and carried Smyth's huge bag of clubs around Portmarnock, the country's most elite golf club, where he was a member. He seemed to be the happiest man at the international tournament, studying yardage charts and advising Smyth on club selection. When he saw his photograph splashed across the front pages of the newspapers the next morning, he was horrified. Dunne had thought that the photographers wouldn't recognise him and, like himself, they would be more interested in big names like Seve Ballesteros. He rang Des Smyth, apologised and withdrew as his caddie.

Haughey postponed his promised reshuffle of the front bench in early 1991 in the wake of the anger within the parliamentary party at the sacking of Brian Lenihan. His instincts told him that Albert Reynolds was awaiting an opportunity to take over as leader. Haughey dismissed Reynolds and his followers as the 'country and western wing', and took an opportunity at an EC summit in Rome to humiliate him. At the final press conference he was joined by his Minister for Finance, Albert Reynolds. In answer to a question about British economic policy, Haughey replied, 'We all know that Chancellors of the Exchequer and Ministers for Finance are neurotic and exotic creatures whose political judgement is not always the best.' Reynolds was deeply hurt by the humiliation, but Haughey continued to praise the 'wonderful job', Reynolds' predecessor, Ray MacSharry, who had become the EC Agricultural Commissioner was doing for Ireland.

Maybe Haughey was whistling past the graveyard when he said he hoped to lead the party into the next election. A week before the Fianna Fáil Ard Fheis in March, Richard Branson flew into Dublin and illegally sold condoms over the counter at his Virgin Megastore in Dublin. The law stated they should only be sold in a chemist shop which Haughey's advisers agreed was ludicrous and spoke of a liberal agenda to regularise the sale of condoms, introduce divorce legislation and decriminalise homosexual acts between consenting adult men. After Mary Robinson's election, it seemed that Fianna Fáil had found its liberal conscience. When it was discussed at cabinet, only two ministers backed Haughey's new liberal agenda.

In May, a Granada television programme, *World In Action*, exposed malpractices at the Goodman beef processing plants. This led to uproar in the Dáil and Haughey was reluctant to agree to set up a judicial tribunal to inquire into the allegations. Reynolds spent the summer preparing for his leadership challenge. Padraig Flynn, who had been a key plotter against Jack Lynch when Haughey assumed the leadership 11 years before, canvassed support for Albert Reynolds from backbenchers. A series of business scandals were reported in the media that autumn, beginning with a controversy at the first State company to be privatised, Greencore. The managing director resigned within days and the chairman, Bernie Cahill, a friend of Haughey's and a chairman of Feltrim Mining, a company established by his son, Conor Haughey, came under pressure. Another scandal, where the State-owned Telecom Éireann bought a site for £9.4 million soon after it had been bought for less than half that price, involved another friend of Haughey's, stockbroker

Dermot Desmond. On 27 September 1991, four Fianna Fáil backbenchers issued a statement criticising Haughey's handling of the scandals.

The Fine Gael leader, John Bruton, disclosed that a confidential report which had been prepared by Dermot Desmond's company for Irish Helicopters, a subsidiary of Aer Lingus, had been delivered to Celtic Helicopters, owned by Ciaran Haughey, the Taoiseach's son. A further row about a land deal at Carysfort and another controversy about a wind generator installed by the ESB on Haughey's island, Inishvickillane, led to a no confidence motion on 16 October. It was Bertie Ahern's skilful negotiating skills which delivered a pay deal with the unions for the government and saved Haughey. To show his gratitude, Haughey described Ahern as '... the most skilful, the most devious and the most cunning.' Ahern sighed and said 'God, that's all I need'.

A special meeting of the Fianna Fáil parliamentary party was called for Saturday, 9 November to discuss the motion of no confidence in Haughey. But even before they turned up for the meeting at 11.30 that morning, Reynolds and his supporters knew they didn't have the numbers. By two o'clock the following morning, Haughey had survived again, by 44 votes to 33.

The week after his trial by party, Charles Haughey received a telephone call in the late afternoon from Ben Dunne who had been playing golf. Earlier, Dunne's solicitor, Noel Smyth, had given him three bank drafts, each for £70,000 and made payable to fictitious names, T. Scott, G. Montgomery and M. Blair. Ben Dunne hadn't left them in his locker when he changed to play at Baltray, and he was aware of them in his pocket when he was taking out his tees and scorecard on the golf course. When he had finished playing, he rang Haughey and said he might call in and have a cup of tea with him on the way home. The Taoiseach looked wretched, old and depressed, the twinkle of mischief gone from his eyes. 'He looked down, a broken man,' said Ben. Dunne's son had just had a kidney transplant, Haughey enquired about the boy's health and they made small talk and Ben got up to leave. According to Dunne, on the way out, he dug his hand into his pocket, pulled out the three bank drafts and said, 'Look, that's something for yourself.' 'Thanks, big fella,' replied the Taoiseach.

At least T. Scott, M. Montgomery and M. Blair didn't lose out. Ben Dunne later admitted they were sort of imaginary friends. But why would he be carrying around three bank drafts, drawn from an Isle of Man bank made out to to people who didn't exist? In a Statement of Claim he made to the High Court in September 1994, Ben Dunne claimed that the three drafts were intended for Margaret, Frank and Therese. It wasn't an isolated occurrence either. He alleged that certain family members ignored the conditions of the trust and used the assets as they wished. He said that some of the directors instructed him to pay money into overseas bank accounts which was then transferred into accounts which were beneficially owned by some of the directors but held in fictitious names. He alleged that Frank Dunne instructed him to pay £650,000 from a Hong Kong-registered company called Carica Ltd into an account in an unnamed Swiss bank. He also said that Frank Dunne received regular payments from two Dunnes Stores accounts held at the Ulster Bank at College Green in Dublin. He claimed that Margaret Heffernan instructed him from time to time to make payments to her from another Hong Kong-registered company,Wytrex. And he also alleged that bank drafts made out in fictitious names were lodged to an account held by her in the Bank of Ireland branch in O'Connell Street in Dublin.

Ben Dunne claimed the name that she used was 'Caroline Dunne' and that special arrangements were made with the bank for the handling and processing of that account. He also said that Therese Dunne had instructed him to make payments from bank accounts held by Wytrex to bank accounts held in her name. He claimed that Therese also received bank drafts and cheques made out in fictitious names which were either lodged into accounts in her name, or 'lodged into an account controlled by Ms Heffernan and transferred into an account who the ultimate beneficiary was Mrs Therese Dunne.' He also alleged that payment for Therese Dunne's American Express card account was 'discharged from accounts of companies within the Dunnes Stores Group.' All allegations of impropriety were vigorously denied by Frank Dunne, Margaret Heffernan and Therese Dunne and later Ben Dunne withdrew his allegations. (Sources close to Ben Dunne claimed in October 1997 that all the family directors in Dunnes Stores were paid an annual salary of £1.5 million plus bonuses from the late 1980s.)

But the three £70,000 drafts just wouldn't go away, and later they would become Charles Haughey's nemesis. In early December, Haughey met the British Prime Minister, John Major, for the first formal Anglo-Irish summit he had attended for eleven years. The Taoiseach liked Major, who unlike other British prime ministers, was refreshingly unpatronising, according to Haughey.

In January 1992, Sean Doherty, who had served as his Minister for Justice in 1982 and had been disgraced for authorising the bugging of two journalists' telephones, appeared on an RTÉ television programme,

Nighthawks. It was a talk show set in a café and usually catered for more esoteric fare than an ageing politician who was the Cathaoirleach of the Senate. They brought the show to Doherty's home county, Roscommon and he delivered a carefully-worded death warrant to Haughey. Asked about the phone tapping scandal, Doherty said, 'There was a decision taken in cabinet that the leaking from cabinet must be stopped. I, as Minister for Justice, had a direct responsibility for doing that; I did that. I do feel I was let down by the fact that people knew what I was doing.' Other ministers in the 1982 government, including Des O'Malley, said phone tapping had never been discussed at cabinet.

Doherty waited a week then called a press conference at the Montrose Hotel, near RTÉ, in Dublin. He was blunt. 'I am confirming tonight that the Taoiseach, Charles J. Haughey, was fully aware, in 1982, that two journalists' phones were being tapped, and he at no stage expressed a reservation about this action. I did not seek nor did I get instruction from any member of the cabinet in this regard, nor did I tell the cabinet that this action had been taken. Telephone tapping was never discussed at cabinet. However, as soon as the transcripts from the taps became available, I took them personally to Mr Haughey in his office and left them in his possession.' Haughey vigorously denied Doherty's allegations.

One of the lessons of the Gulf War was that in modern warfare soldiers are more likely to be casualties of friendly fire than enemy flak, and it was a Fianna Fáil TD, Sean Power, who had told Haughey, 'The people of Ireland are disgusted with the scandals and the relationship you, Taoiseach, have with some of the people at the centre of those scandals.' Haughey was like some exhausted old heavyweight boxer who had taken so many blows he could be knocked over by a political flyweight like Doherty. Worse was to come: an opinion poll showed more people believed Sean Doherty's claim than Haughey's denial. Besides, the Progressive Democrats threatened to call a general election if he didn't resign, just as they had threatened to pull down his government before Haughey had sacked his oldest friend, Brian Lenihan. He resigned as Taoiseach and retired as Leader of Fianna Fáil on 7 February 1992, just a week before his friend and benefactor, Ben Dunne, went off on a golfing holiday to Florida.

GRIFFITH COLLEGE CORK
Cove Street,
Sullivan's Quay, Cork.
Tel. +353 - 21 - 450 7027
Fax. +353 - 21 - 4507659
www.gcc.ie

Chapter Nine

In the early 1990s, the style journalists on British magazines who fashion themselves as social anthropologists, discovered New Lads. It was just a new name for old bad habits: self-absorbed young males dedicating themselves to hell-raising and hedonism, sport and sex. The promotion of the New Lad was a reaction to the New Man of the 1980s who cooked, hoovered and shared homemaking responsibilities with a partner who demanded an equal say with equal pay.

If he had been 20 years younger and eight kilograms lighter in 1992, Ben Dunne would have been a New Lad. But then, Ben was the original of the species, a red meat-eater who believed the sporting element of business and the business side of sport should be exclusively male preserves. Long before either the New Man or the New Lad, the Man's Man bonded with his boardroom peers on the golf course while he kept his Stepford wife or girlfriend in a separate compartment. A Man's Man would justify this behaviour as genetically inherited from a time when men hunted for lunch in packs and celebrated the kill together.

For the previous three years, Dunne had organised golf trips to Florida in February for himself and his friends to soak up the sun and escape the dreary winter and post-Christmas dip in business at home. There would usually be around a dozen of them, mostly businessmen, whose company he enjoyed. It was innocent enough: play golf, top up their tans, have a few beers and a laugh. Ben's etiquette meant talking business was out of bounds on the course, any mention of deals or trade was strictly forbidden, yet side bets for the price of a small family car were okay so long as they related to the game.

The gang had already been to Tarpon Springs on Florida's Gulf Coast, when someone told him he should check out the world-class golf courses in Orlando. His travel agent in Dublin booked 11 first-class seats on a British Airways flight from London on Saturday 15 February with ten single rooms plus a deluxe suite in Stouffers Resort Hotel. Ten of the party travelled from Ireland to join the British Airways flight in London. On an impulse, Ben, who was playing golf in Jersey, asked a taxi-driver who had driven him around the island, to collect his passport and accompany him on a flight to London where they both joined the party headed to Florida.

Orlando is dominated by Disneyworld, the mecca for perfect couples with beautiful blonde children. Where the universal language of 'have a nice day' Disneyspeak is delivered with a smile in a southern drawl. One of the wealthiest cities in the United States, it is the most popular tourist destination in the world where each sunny day awakes to a dawn chorus of chirpy optimism. Orlando endlessly espouses family values and the pursuit of happiness through vigorous outdoor activities.

Ben checked into his $500-a-night suite on the tenth floor at the huge Stouffers complex, and spoke to a concierge in the lobby, a sort of Mr Fixit for guests, who could usually get reservations in busy restaurants and tickets for sold-out shows. One of the concierges on duty that Saturday evening had a price list for pleasures not listed in the hotel directory.

Ben wanted female company and a big bag of cocaine. The female company was just an hour and a phone call away. Cindy Mitchell, a former dancer, had put on too much weight to wear a purple spandex mini dress, a white sequinned bustier with very high heels and not look conspicuous. She was 32 years old, wore a long blonde wig and had a butterfly tattooed on her right breast. She must have turned heads sashaying through the lobby to the elevators and up to suite 1044. Ben Dunne answered her knock on the door wearing a white towelling robe bearing the hotel's logo and a gold Rolex watch.

An experienced woman in a dangerous profession, she insisted on seeing his passport and noticed 'Bernard' had a lot of US entry stamps. He told her to call him Ben and lied that he had just flown in from New Jersey on a company Lear jet. She admired his watch and he took it off and showed it to her with a cautionary tale: he said another woman had been attracted to his watch and asked him to let her wear it, hoping he would forget about it. Cindy knew he was very rich, but she also thought he was a bit naive. After a chaste talk, where he discussed the golf course at Barnett Creek Country Club, Ben asked her to bring a friend to a party he was planning for Monday night.

The weather was Florida perfect the next morning and the party of 12 were taken to Barnett Creek in a bus. The golf was good, they were bussed back to the hotel and in the evening they broke up into small groups and had a meal, then a drink before bed. It was an eclectic group: Noel Fox, a trustee of Dunnes Stores who had arranged to pay the ransom when Ben was kidnapped 11 years before, was there. A future Mayor of Galway, John Mulholland, an old friend of Ben's, made the trip.

Businessmen Jimmy McCormick, Peter Henshaw, Niall Clarkin, Mickey Heaslip, Norman Taylor, Declan O'Callaghan, and Tony Gray, a professional golfer. Des Smyth, who had been on previous trips to Florida with Ben couldn't make it to Orlando, but his caddy, John O'Reilly, was there and, of course, the surprise guest, 'Jim' Hawkins, the taxi-driver from Jersey.

Detectives believe the concierge delivered the huge cellophane bag of cocaine, at least 40 grammes, in the late afternoon or evening on the Monday. Later, Cindy Mitchell returned to suite 1044 with a friend, Andrea Nathanson, also 32 years old, and she wore a blonde wig too, although hers was short and curly which showed off her long dangling earrings.

On this visit, Ben Dunne was sniffing huge amounts of cocaine and couldn't stop talking. He told the women he had inherited the largest manufacturing business in Ireland from his father, which made him a billionaire. People cheat you in business, he said, and then he rambled on about the Catholic Church and confession. He spoke about his kidnapping in 1981 and said it was a horrible experience, according to Cindy Mitchell. Taking line after line of cocaine, he showed symptoms of paranoia, paced the room continually and told the women not to leave his sight, he even insisted on leaving the bathroom door open. Eventually, Dunne asked Andrea Nathanson to leave because she was fidgeting so much. He was terrified about his money and kept muttering, 'watch the dimes and the dollars will look after themselves.' Cindy Mitchell told him to lay off the white stuff and kissed him goodbye.

After another day at Barnett Creek Country Club on Tuesday, the golfers were bussed back to Stouffers and Ben went off to his room after dinner. Cindy Mitchell rang him in the suite and he said to come over, but when she arrived, Ben had a friend with him. She described him as having blonde hair, bad teeth and a Russian wedding ring on the ring finger of his right hand. Cindy Mitchell says Ben was strung out on cocaine again and she left. She kept a souvenir of the encounter: a $300 credit card slip bearing the imprint Bernard M. Dunne.

Ben was getting bored with Stouffers and the daily bus trips to the golf course, and decided to move the party to the most expensive hotel in the area. On the Tuesday morning, he rang the Grand Cypress Hotel, which he knew from previous stays there had two golf courses in its grounds. He booked the accommodation, all of which was to be charged to his Bank of Ireland credit card. The Irish party left their luggage in their rooms at Stouffers when they went out to play golf on Wednesday morning and were assured it would be unpacked when they arrived in their rooms in the Grand Cypress in the late afternoon.

Again, all the others had single rooms, each costing $255 dollars a night, and Ben took a suite on the seventeenth floor, with a daily rate of $1,200 plus ten per cent sales tax. He didn't appear to be especially depressed or upset that evening when the others drifted off in threes and fours for dinner in the hotel dining-rooms. Ben was asked to eat with several of them, but he said he was going for a quiet drink. He went to the split-level suite alone, watched television, then an in-house movie. He rang home most days and caught up on the gossip about his friend, Charles Haughey, who had retired a week before they left for Florida. Presumably bored and looking for more exciting company, he flicked through the yellow pages of the Orlando telephone directory. There were 63 advertisements for escort services but he was attracted to a full-page advert on page 528, headed 'Escorts In A Flash – We Can Be With You In An Hour'.

He rang the agency sometime before midnight. They called him back and he agreed to pay $300 for two hours with a female escort. He was told the women are then free to make any further private arrangement directly with the customer. A man employed by the agency called Eric, known as 'The Enforcer', called to Dunne's room and collected the $300 in cash, in advance. The agency left a message on the pager of Denise Wojcik, one of their escorts, who shared a trailer with a friend, Delta Rittenhouse, who had introduced her room-mate to the escort service, and Delta's nine-month-old baby, Brittany.

Locals blamed the residents of the trailer park on Powhatton Road where Denise lived for an upsurge of crime in the area, and called them welfare scroungers and trailer trash. This angered Ms Wojcik, who had lost her job as a librarian six months before and received just $45 of the $150 an hour minimum fee the agency charged its clients. She worked four or five times a week for the agency but vehemently denied that any prostitution was involved.

Denise Wojcik was already driving the 25 miles along Interstate 4 when a message from the agency on her pager confirmed that 'The Enforcer' had collected the money. It was half past one in the morning when Ben Dunne greeted her at the door of suite 1708 with a glass of chilled Dom Perignon champagne and a $400 tip. Fifteen minutes later they were sniffing cocaine and then Dunne led her up the winding staircase connecting the living-room to the bedroom and en suite bathroom. She later told police they must have consumed more than 50 lines of cocaine. The cocaine was in a cellophane bag on a nightstand. She slipped out of the blue cotton print dress, they got into a bath together and he chopped up cocaine with a plastic K Club membership card and laid out lines on the edge of the double tub bath. They sniffed it through a rolled up $100 dollar bill until it became soggy and then he used a $20 bill. They were talking non-stop, drinking the champagne and then they drank the contents of the mini bar, including Kahlua mixed with Bailey's Irish Cream and beer. They talked and talked: he told her he was in retailing and spoke about his wife before opening up about sexual fantasies.

Around five o'clock, Denise gave Dunne the phone number of the trailer she shared with Delta Rittenhouse, he rang and asked her to join them. Ms Rittenhouse said she had to look after her baby but would try and get another woman to join them. Dunne and Wojcik continued to drink, snort cocaine and talk. At half past six, another woman who worked with the escort service, Cherie Rudulski, was rung by Delta Rittenhouse and told she would get $300 dollars for two hours and asked to call Denise Wojcik at suite 1708 at the Grand Cypress Hotel, if she was interested.

Ben Dunne went to the safe in his room and tried the combination but it wouldn't open. Paranoid from an overdose of cocaine, his mind began racing and imagining terrible possibilities. He had £4,000 in Irish pounds and nearly $9,000 in bills locked away. He tried again and again to read the number from a crumpled piece of paper but the door remained firmly closed. He began to panic and started pacing up and down the room. Denise Wojcik went up to him and asked if she could help but he put up his hands like a shield and shouted, 'leave me alone, leave me alone'. She tried to calm him down and suggested he call the hotel security to open the safe door. He explained his problem with the combination lock to the hotel security, hung up the phone, and then he jumped on the bed and screamed for her to get out. Still in her underwear after the bath, she went into the bedroom to get dressed. Ben picked up a piece of wood and began swinging it over his head. Later, she told police he was 'like some crazed King Kong, jumping up and down and swinging this object over his head.'

Ben Dunne opened the door of his suite and saw a security man, dressed in a black boilersuit. Dunne panicked, began shouting, 'get the police, get the police' and moved to a corner of the balcony beside a window, close to the edge and looking down 17 floors to a white grand piano in the lobby below. The security men were frightened by Ben Dunne's apparent psychotic behaviour and a maid working in a neighbouring suite rang the hotel switchboard. Four months later, Dunne told journalist Rory Godson, 'I was on the balcony and the police said that Major Marcus wanted to speak to me. I said there were no majors in the police. I was calling for my friends, wondering where they were. They never came. I wanted to stay out in the public view, where they couldn't touch me. I didn't trust the police and I wanted to bring my pals along. I wasn't suicidal. I was fighting to stay alive.'

Denise Wojcik tried to leave, then she went back into the suite when he continued to scream and bellow. A meeting of the senior management staff was nearly finished when the security manager Rick de Treville and assistant manager Courtney Torreyson were informed there was an emergency on the seventeenth floor. Denise Wojcik had made her way to the lobby and told the security manager a man from Ireland had gone mad. It was just after eight o'clock in the morning and the lobby below was filling up with guests either going to breakfast or filing out onto coaches to visit theme parks.

Another group of Irishmen were also staying in suites on the seventeenth floor, the rock group U2, preparing for the first date of a tour of the United States that Saturday night. They were in the lobby, waiting to go to rehearsals in the stadium 20 miles away and witnessed the commotion. Bono, the lead singer, said later he had never witnessed anything like it before. 'It wasn't at all noisy or aggravated,' he said. 'It was ugly and eerie. Everybody was hoping this guy would be okay.' Rick de Treville, the hotel's security manager, thought it was one of the rock musicians who was panicking and asked two of U2's security staff to accompany him to the seventeenth floor. It was after nine o'clock and De Treville realised he had better wait for the police.

Three patrol cars answered the emergency. Deputy Howard Wright and Deputy Sam Spanich arrived at the same time and Deputy Chris Ford a few minutes later. Wright cleared the hotel security staff from the seventeenth floor, while de Treville protested that he was in charge of the area. Deputy Sam Spanich, who just a year before had moved to Orlando after 15 years with the Chicago police, began talking softly to Dunne, now half-crazed, dressed only in his boxer shorts.

Five years after the incident, Deputy Spanich recalled it vividly. 'The way he was acting, I thought he would go and take me with him. He was really paranoid, but we built a bond and I never left his side.' Dunne told Spanich he had been drinking and had taken drugs, then asked about his friends. The rest of the golfing party noticed a commotion in the lobby but didn't connect it to their party or Ben Dunne. 'I had breakfast in my room,' one of them said, 'and I didn't think anything of it. Looking back on it now, I suppose we must look foolish, or thoughtless, but we went out to the golf course and expected Ben to either join us there or follow on later.'

Meanwhile Cherie Rudulski had arrived by cab and noticed three police cars and a fire ambulance outside the Grand Cypress. It was just after eight o'clock and she realised there was no chance of getting to suite 1708 for the $37 to pay the cab driver. She said, 'I had to lose that cab driver fast, but I was wearing a cocktail dress and high heels, which looks odd at that time of the morning, and a policewoman came up to me and said she wanted to speak to me later. I went across the road to a 7-Eleven shop and called Denise on the phone to the suite and I was astonished when she answered it. She said he had flipped out just before eight when he was trying to get money out of the safe. Denise didn't seem too bad then, but I was stuck 20 miles from home with no money. One of the strangest things of that very strange morning was that leaving the hotel I saw Bono of U2 walking past me. I've always been a fan but it hardly seemed the time to introduce myself, and besides, he looked very grim.'

Orange County Sheriff's Office rushed two specialist negotiators to the hotel, Captain La Fort and Major Marcus, along with other back-up teams. But it was Deputy Sam Spanich, 37 years old and the father of three children, who knelt on the balcony and kept talking to Ben Dunne. 'I was looking at Ben and Ben and I were on the ledge. I got into a position where he was closer to the window and I was closer to the edge of the balcony. There were 15 policemen, but he couldn't see any of them. Then five guys grabbed him and handcuffed him. We had to hog-tie him to get him out of the hotel and he struggled on the way to the hospital.'

When they searched him, police found a small bag of cocaine in a pocket in his pants. Mary Dunne, Ben's wife, had phoned the hotel while her husband was on the edge of the balcony and had her call put through to the assistant manager, Courtney Torreyson. She didn't mention the incident, but told Mary Dunne there was something wrong with her husband, that he was very paranoid and asking for the police.

Later, a senior police officer rang Mary Dunne and told her everything about the incident, including the presence of cocaine and a call-girl. Sources later said that when police officers arrested Denise Wojcik, she offered to tell them what was in the room if they let her off. They agreed, if it was good enough. She told them he had a big black bag with lots of cash and a big bag of cocaine. Detective Chris Ford, who had been promoted to plain clothes duties just six months before, usually covered the Disneyworld beat. He had spoken to Denise Wojcik in the lobby and asked a hotel manager to open the door of Ben Dunne's suite. He found the black bag containing a big plastic bag with 32.5 grammes, more than an ounce of cocaine, and $9,738 in cash. It was a bad career day for Detective Chris Ford: not only had he made an illegal search which would prevent the ounce of cocaine he had found in Dunne's room being used in any criminal prosecution, but his car broke down and had to be towed away from the front of the hotel.

The demons summoned up by the cocaine he had snorted on the seventeenth floor were still torturing Ben Dunne as police officers tried to get him through the hotel to the ambulance at the front door. He was hog-tied, cuffed at the wrists and ankles, with policemen supporting each end of a pole, carrying him trussed up like a beast prepared for a barbeque. He continued to stuggle and bellow. Everyone who saw the spectacle agreed there is no less dignified way to leave a public building. It was a surreal scene in the lobby of the Grand Cypress, where the decor theme was of a tropical rain forest, complete with live squawking parrots.

Noel Fox, a lifelong and intimate friend of the family, who had arranged for the ransom to be paid to Ben's kidnappers 11 years before, was on the hotel's championship golf course when he heard the news. He went to his room and called the Irish Embassy in Washington and they recommended Holland and Knight, an Ivy League firm of corporate lawyers, who passed the brief on to Slaughter and Levanthal, an eminent firm of criminal defence lawyers in Florida.

Dunne struggled with police all the way to hospital but Deputy Sam Spanich said he eventually calmed down and realised the enormity of his problems. He had another panic attack in the hospital and had to be further restrained. Dunne later told reporter Rory Godson, 'when anyone in the hospital comes near me, they put on rubber gloves. I know now they were worried about Aids. Then, I thought they were trying not to leave fingerprints on me. I was in a blind fucking panic over those rubber gloves wondering, "if this is a real hospital, why is nobody coming to see me? Why is no one telephoning me?"' At 11 o'clock he was discharged from Sand Lake hospital and taken to Orange County Jail and ordered to wear a prison uniform.

The police knew they had a problem. Deputy Howard Wright, the arresting officer, refused to charge Dunne with trafficking even when more senior officers said the huge quantity of cocaine justified it. Aware of the circumstances in which his less experienced colleague, Detective Chris Ford, had searched his room, Wright was worried. Eventually

Sergeant Barbara Lewis directly ordered Wright to charge Dunne with trafficking. Dunne told Rory Godson, 'I hadn't slept for two days. It was 6 p.m. Then they said they were taking me to see my lawyer. I go into a room and this guy walks in, chewing gum and says: "I'm your lawyer. My name is Slaughter. Butch Slaughter." Jesus Christ.' Dunne was released on $25,000 bail put up by Mr Snapp, a local bondsman. He couldn't return to the Grand Cypress, but headed to another hotel where he had another meeting with his lawyer, Mr Slaughter and got the $25,000 to repay Mr Snapp, the bail bondsman who held his passport.

The rest of the golfing party couldn't believe it when they returned to the hotel and heard the gory details of Big Ben's apocalypse on the seventeenth floor. Some of them managed to get flights out of Orlando that same evening, others flew direct to London the next day. On Friday, Bono phoned U2's manager, Paul McGuinness, in Dublin and told him a Dublin guy called Dunne had been arrested at the hotel with cocaine. Both of them assumed it was a member of another Dunne family from Dublin, with a long association with crime and narcotics, who was involved.

Before he left Orlando on the Saturday morning, Ben Dunne rang his wife Mary and she gave him more bad news: *The Sunday Tribune* had the details of his incident in the Grand Cypress. He flew to London and, travelling under an assumed name, arrived in Dublin early on Sunday morning. As he expected, the news of his disgrace had hit the streets of Dublin on Saturday night, splashed over the front page of *The Sunday Tribune*. The headline was staring at Ben Dunne from the news-stands when he arrived at Dublin airport on Sunday morning. He told reporter Godson, 'I came home and lay down on the bed thinking about it. I told Mary all the details. Five minutes later the press arrived and I had to deal with it.'

Dunne's solicitor and mentor, Noel Smyth, was staying at a cottage in Loughrea, County Galway, for a weekend's fishing when a doctor friend rang him on the Sunday morning and told him: 'Your big pal is all over *The Sunday Tribune*.' Smyth, who had acted for Dunne since 1987, immediately rang him at his home in Dublin and Dunne said: 'Where the fuck are you? Get back up here quick.'

Dunne's home in Castleknock was surrounded by journalists when his solicitor arrived that afternoon. Ben Dunne was contrite. He had to face his wife and immediate family and then his siblings. Margaret, his older sister, was likely to be angry at the public humiliation of the family name. But first he had to deal with the public: Noel Smyth advised him to do a *mea culpa*, blame no one but himself, tell the full truth, apologise publicly and face the consequences.

The Dunne family trust which was worth some £600 million in February 1992, and had an estimated annual turnover of some £900 million from its 51 stores in the Republic, Northern Ireland and England. They were the richest family in Ireland, private almost to the point of paranoia; they had always been deeply suspicious of the media and deeply detested any form of personal publicity. Twenty years before, Ben Dunne Senior, who began building the family retailing empire in 1944, was asked his opinion on newspapers. 'Why people read newspapers is that they've nothing else to do, and they think it eases their tension ... like drinking,' he replied. Against two generations of precedent and his own strong inclinations, Ben Dunne took Smyth's advice and called a press conference at his home that Sunday evening. He even gave a television interview for RTÉ news. He wore an open-neck shirt, a dark jacket and his hair was unkempt. He looked weary, dejected and badly in need of a confessor. He spoke softly, acknowledged the hurt he had caused to his family and said his arrest was 'something I will overcome'.

Explaining that he had not attempted suicide, Dunne said he had suffered a panic attack after taking cocaine. Although past experiences, including his kidnapping in 1981, had been factors, he said he could not blame the past for his drug-taking which had put his job 'in jeopardy'. 'I can blame no one but myself. No, I'm not a cocaine user, in a weak moment I took the goddamn stuff and in no way am I looking for pity. I took it, I shouldn't have taken it. Just the same way, I am not an alcoholic. I took cocaine and I won't be taking it again. It was hard to be arrested as a dealer, but it is something I will overcome. I was weak and that is why I took it. If the situation arose where it came up again, I wouldn't do it again. I am admitting that nobody put a gun to my head to make me take cocaine. I had a free choice about whether to break the law or not. I am not addicted to any drugs, legal or otherwise. There is an awful lot of prescribed drugs that I wouldn't take. I don't drink shorts, I drink beer. I am not interested in drinking shorts because I'm afraid to. I have caused a lot of hardship to my wife and kids.'

He said the incident had '... cost me dear. I have hurt a lot of people including myself'. Like any manager in Dunnes Stores, he had put his job in jeopardy by taking drugs. He said he was not trying to commit suicide when he stood on the seventeenth floor balcony of his hotel in Orlando, but he didn't believe the bona fides of the hotel's security staff, and when he looked for his friends they weren't there. 'The main reason for the panic was that I had taken substances I shouldn't have, but in normal circumstances when somebody arrives at the front door I look for identification and I look out of the peephole of the hotel room. The past experiences have a bearing on me, but I can't blame past experiences,' he said.

It was a *tour de force*, particularly the television interview where he appeared to bare his soul and bear the consequences. Overnight, there was a rush of public sympathy to him, confounding professional public relations consultants who, in the past, had urged public figures in difficulties to deal with the media through an intermediary. The Dunne family had a bad reputation as employers and received a lot of negative media coverage over their attitude to staff relations through the years. They were perceived as *nouveau riche*, trade union-busting bullies after the prolonged strike over the importation of South African oranges in 1984. Yet Ben Dunne's emotional confession on television and in newspapers did more to restore their reputation than any slick public relations campaign.

Back in Orlando, Slaughter and Levanthal were preparing Ben Dunne's defence on charges of trafficking cocaine. Butch Slaughter had the reputation to match a name straight out of pulp fiction, and like his partner Robert Levanthal, he had earned a formidable reputation as a federal prosecutor. As gamekeepers turned poachers, they had built a very successful practice as criminal defence lawyers based in an opulent suite of offices in the business district of Orlando. An Assistant District Attorney assigned to the Dunne case said, 'they come expensive, or they don't come at all'.

A sergeant from the Orange County Sherriff's Office interviewed the concierge who had supplied the woman and cocaine for Ben Dunne in Stouffers Hotel. They were satisfied that Dunne paid considerably over the street market price for the narcotics but without corroborating evidence couldn't charge him with any offence. After a preliminary investigation, and a quiet acknowledgement that the seizure of the 32.5 grams of cocaine in Dunne's hotel suite was illegal, Slaughter and Levanthal, instructed by Noel Smyth in Dublin, prepared to plea bargain with the Distrct Attorney.

Noel Smyth flew to Orlando where Slaughter and Levanthal had arranged for him to be appointed Attorney in Fact, which gives the authority of power of attorney, and authorised him to make an agreement in Ben Dunne's name. Smyth even visited the county prison in Orlando and was horrified by what he saw. When he returned, Smyth began a protracted correspondence with Circuit Judge, Dorothy J. Russell, who was hearing the case. It was decided to send Judge Russell character references from a variety of people in the sporting world, business community and others involved in charity work. They wanted to show her that Dunne was an upstanding citizen who had suffered post-traumatic stress syndrome related to his kidnapping 11 years before. The professional golfers, Des Smyth and Christy O'Connor Junior, wrote letters, so did his accountant Noel Fox, and 20 Dunnes Stores employees also wrote character references to the judge. One of the letters, available in Dunne's file in the public record office in Orlando, from John Small, 80 years old and the longest-serving employee of the company in Northern Ireland, was particularly moving.

Noel Smyth sent Judge Russell details of the Charter Clinic in London where he proposed that Dunne be treated in their alcohol and drug unit programme. On 1 May 1992, the court dropped the charges of trafficking cocaine and accepted Dunne's guilty plea to possession of a small amount of cocaine. He was fined $5,000 dollars and undertook to go into residential evaluation for 'no less than 28 days' and remain under the supervision of Dr Jeffrey A. Danziger for a year. Both Dr Danziger and Noel Smyth were required to report to the court about his progress.

Ben Dunne entered the Charter Group Clinic on 1 June but there were rumblings in the board room at Dunnes Stores despite a public display of business as usual. Just a few days later, Noel Smyth took a call on his analogue mobile phone from Margaret Heffernan. He was driving in from Dublin airport and heading through Phoenix Park and the call broke up. She rang back and attacked Smyth for having a bad influence and asked if he didn't realise the harm he was doing to Ben, that the Charter Group Clinic was only a glorified hotel and six months in prison would have done Ben a world of good. However their conversation was monitored by someone with a scanner and the details were released to the media. They were the preliminary exchanges in the most bitter family feud in the history of Irish business, and there would be other casualties caught in the crossfire, including a former Taoiseach and a serving cabinet minister.

After a month in the clinic, Ben Dunne took his family abroad on holiday. A board meeting was called for 16 July. Frank Dunne proposed a new set of rules to run the company, they were seconded by Margaret Heffernan and agreed by Therese and Elizabeth McMahon. At the end of July when he returned, Ben was advised by his lawyer, Noel Smyth, that Frank and Margaret were moving to get him out. Although he was acting chairman, he needed to be formally voted into the position and he was supported by both Elizabeth and Therese. The Back-to-School sale in the autumn of 1992 was a disappointment and Ben thought the company needed to get back to basics and bought cheap jeans and shirts from Asian suppliers in Britain. Some of the stock didn't even carry the St Bernard label, but it sold well in the stores in Britain and he introduced the bargain range to the Irish stores.

When supplies ran out, he decided to buy directly from manufacturers and flew out first class with Qantas to Singapore in November with Noel Smyth, where they spent six days at the Shangri-La hotel meeting suppliers and visiting factories. They hired an aircraft to visit other factories and spent four days at the Hyatt hotel in Bali before returning. They ordered £20 million worth of goods, but it had to be confirmed by a letter of credit within 14 days of the goods being ready for delivery. Ben showed samples to the board in January 1993 on his return and Margaret proposed a vote of thanks for his enterprise. Later, she would call his discount purchases in Britain 'a buying spree'.

In February 1993, a year after the Florida debacle, Frank Dunne moved against him with Margaret's support, and his long standing ally, Therese, backed them. Elizabeth remained loyal to him, but Ben Dunne was out-voted three to two and removed as chairman. He rang Noel Fox, a trustee, and said he would take a settlement of £10 million plus the store in Waterford, but his offer was refused. Frustrated and angry, Ben paid £900,000 for Dunloe House, a publicly-quoted company, and planned to open a chain of Buy Right Stores selling clothing, with his wife Mary. He had already been effectively stripped of all executive power shortly before Elizabeth McMahon, his only supporter on the board, died unexpectedly in July. Ben thought the shock of Elizabeth's death might lead to a reconciliation or a settlement within a couple of months. Meanwhile, everyone who worked closely with Ben in Dunnes Stores was either moved sideways, demoted or fired.

Ben Dunne and Noel Smyth then went to war and began litigation to break up the family trust. Ben said it was a sham, that the trust was never intended to be 'a bona fide discretionary trust' and that certain family members ignored the conditions of the trust and used the assets as they wished. In response, Dunnes Stores commissioned a report from independent auditors, Price Waterhouse, to investigate and report on Ben's business dealings when he ran the company.

Chapter Ten

After the experiences of a celebrity American gangster and a fugitive British peer, any Irish politician saddled with the sobriquet 'Lucky' should have been wary. Maybe the cool clean hero of Fine Gael thought Luciano was simply the first name of a fat Italian tenor, or that Lucan is just a village west of Dublin, but he didn't demur when his colleagues called him 'Lucky Lowry'. After all, he was a farm boy from rural Ireland with modest academic achievements yet he had secured a senior place at the heart of government. Popular with the people who elected him, attractive to women and leading the life of a millionaire as a successful businessman, what was he, if not lucky?

Michael Lowry was a key negotiator for the senior party in forming the Rainbow Coalition government in 1994. He was the Taoiseach's most trusted political adviser, one of John Bruton's close personal friends. In office, he demanded the highest ethical standards in both government and business; some spoke of him as a future Taoiseach. Hadn't he been relegated to sit in the back of a smaller car when he moved from his personal top-of-the-range BMW to the government-supplied Mercedes after he was appointed a member of the government? Didn't he live in one of the finest period houses in Tipperary recently refurbished at enormous expense? Wasn't he a source of great pride to his family and friends? Didn't his enemies envy his phenomenal success? Lucky? The way Michael Lowry saw it, he had had won the Lotto of life.

On 15 December 1994, John Bruton appointed Michael Lowry as Minister for Transport, Energy and Communications. The farmer's son from rural Tipperary had arrived at the heart of government, in the most important economic ministry held by Fine Gael, responsible for ten State-owned companies with a combined annual budget of more than £2 billion. On 1 January 1995, *The Sunday Business Post* declared: 'It has all come good for Michael Lowry ... his ambition to be the next leader of Fine Gael is firmly on course'.

One of his first decisions as a minister was to appoint a public relations consultant, Bill O'Herlihy, a former party activist with long experience of, and significant success in, the black arts of political spin doctoring. Lowry hit the ground running, mapping out an ambitious programme and resolving to sort out the problems in the State-owned companies within a year. He saw the ESB and Telecom as his priorities. By March 1995, he had outlined the conditions for the government's granting of a licence for the second mobile phone service to operate in competition to the existing State-owned service. It would be the biggest contract ever to be awarded to a private company in the history of the State.

In what would become the hallmark of Lowry's machismo ministerial style, he replaced Dermot O'Leary, a Fianna Fáil activist, as non-executive chairman of CIE. O'Leary's denial of any conflict between him and the minister was unconvincing and Fianna Fáil's shadow spokesman, Seamus Brennan, said O'Leary had been removed 'in a nakedly political' manner. Eamonn Walsh, the respected and highly-regarded retiring chief executive of Hibernian Insurance, was asked by Lowry to take up a position as executive chairman of CIE which needed state intervention of £109 million the previous year.

That same week, O'Leary found himself publicly denying accusations that he had abused his position in CIE, obviously inspired by leaks to the press from anonymous sources close to the minister. In May, the Fine Gael Minister of Defence, Hugh Coveney, resigned when it was revealed that he had phoned the chairman of Bord Gáis, Michael Conlon, in mid-April asking if the quantity surveying consultancy in which he had been a partner, would be able to tender for a £6 million contract at the State company's headquarters on Albert Road in Cork.

Lowry was outraged and accused Fianna Fáil supporters of leaking the information to a Sunday newspaper. Although Coveney's resignation was an admission of at least carelessness, if not culpability, on his part, Lowry instigated an inquiry demanding to know if the leaking of Coveney's conversation with Conlon was a breach of the Code of Conduct for board members. Fine Gaelers roared approval at Lowry's confrontational style: he was, they said, beating Fianna Fáil at their own game and building a reputation as a cool, clean and fearless hero within his own party. In early July, he faced down a revolt of five Fianna Fáil-appointed directors of CIE and humiliated Seamus Brennan, the party's spokesman who had championed their cause. Bill O'Herlihy, his public relations consultant, ensured Lowry's triumphs were prominently reported in the media.

Through June and July of 1995 strange anonymous letters, written in ball-point pen on ruled A4 buff-coloured pages, were sent to the Taoiseach, the Minister for Justice, the Attorney General, and, curiously, the recently demoted minister, Hugh Coveney. As a journalist who had been chronicling Michael Lowry's performance in government, I also received a series of these anonymous letters, signed 'D. Whelan'. They contained details of alleged corruption in the State companies and gave the bank account numbers of the people involved. The letters also named individuals the author claimed were involved in elaborate tax evasion schemes and gave dates when false passports were allegedly used for foreign travel.

The contents were too convincing, the language and grammar too precise, to dismiss them totally as the work of a crank. Some of the detail in the letters hadn't been reported in the media, but checks confirmed some of the facts to be accurate. Then one six page letter dated 17 July claimed two businessmen 'have hired a private eye to check into the private lives of Lowry; Eamon Walsh Ch/man & Michael O'Donnell chief executive of CIE' and went on to make scandalous allegations about them.

It was a sensational story: the prospect of a senior government minister being secretly observed by private detectives, or anyone, was a sinister development in Irish public life and posed a potentially serious security threat. On 26 July, a week after receiving the letter, I approached Michael Lowry outside the self-service restaurant in Leinster House and asked him if he knew he was under surveillance. As casually as if he was discussing the weather, Lowry said he was aware of it, that the gardaí were investigating the matter, but it was a delicate matter, a woman was involved, and would I please hold off writing the story until the following week? He assured me that no one else would get the story but he wanted to get the report of the garda investigation before it became public. I agreed to postpone writing the story until the following Tuesday.

The story appeared four days later in the *Sunday Independent* where, without qualification, it said: 'The Taoiseach has been told that Transport and Communications Minister Michael Lowry is under surveillance by criminal elements attempting to prevent a clampdown on corruption in the semi-state sector.' It claimed that gardaí were investigating 'evidence' that Dublin businessmen were behind it, that the Garda Commissioner had been handed 'documentary evidence' and that he had been personally briefed by the Minister for Justice. Mr Lowry had refused to comment, although he and other senior politicians were said to be 'gravely concerned at the threat to the government'.

The story was further inflamed by the onset of the traditional news famine in August, the silly season. Michael Lowry was portrayed as a martyred minister, subjected to personal vilification by criminals controlled by sinister businessmen because of his heroic efforts to clean up corruption. In an off-the-record briefing, sources close to Lowry even named a thoroughly reputable security company, run by a Fianna Fáil activist, which, they claimed, was conducting the surveillance.

Coming at a time when Dublin was suffering a wave of serious crime and murder, the air was thick with ugly rumours, allegations and counter-claims. An editorial in *The Irish Times* called for new laws to root out 'Sicilian' levels of corruption in Irish public life. Lowry's skilful public relations consultants worked overtime, earning their £50,000 a year fees paid from the public purse to promote the minister's cause. The story also attracted writs from Cork property developer, Owen O'Callaghan, and former CIE chairman, Dermot O'Leary, who claimed they had been defamed by the Minister. Bill O'Herlihy, Lowry's media adviser, referred a statement from Fianna Fáil to his legal advisers.

Then it emerged that the only evidence to support Lowry's claim that he was under surveillance was the anonymous letters. Wary of being drawn into a political controversy, the gardaí issued a Jesuitical statement saying that because it was not illegal to put anyone, including a government minister, under surveillance, no law was broken, and, therefore, no investigation was required. Some journalists thought the statement was too clever by half and deeply disingenuous: If the gardaí had been informed that the minister was under covert surveillance and they had not checked it out because surveillance was not illegal, what would have happened if any harm had befallen Lowry? Resignations would have been expected in the highest ranks of the Gardaí.

Some journalists were told that it wasn't Lowry, but a married woman with whom he was spending time, who had been the subject of surveillance by private detectives hired by her husband. However in off-the-record briefings, senior Garda officers said they had thoroughly investigated the claims but could find no evidence of any surveillance on the minister. Another detective confided that many of the private detective agencies employed either retired, or off-duty, gardaí and they had all been approached, but none of the security firms or private detectives knew anything about surveillance on Michael Lowry. The gardaí were determined not to be drawn into any political scandal.

The minister had no doubts, and said it was efforts by him to smash a sinister group of Dublin businessmen trading with the semi-state sector that led to the surveillance operation on his private and commercial life. After the initial public sympathy for his apparent determination to root out corruption, and the torrent of favourable publicity in the media, weeks dragged by without any convincing evidence being produced. Inevitably, the media became impatient waiting for some tangible proof to back up the minister's astonishing allegations. When nothing was forthcoming, he inevitably fell under a cloud of suspicion and became the target of ridicule and damaging rumours. His credibility as a government minister was being questioned by other politicians, including colleagues in his own party.

The first plan was to call a press conference to announce the formation of a task force to advise on cleaning up the semi-state companies and deal with the outstanding issues. Then someone must have remembered Lowry's poverty of language and lack of grace under pressure. Rather than risk a free-for-all press conference and awkward, searching questions, his media advisers changed the format to a series of one-to-one briefings where the minister met representatives of each newspaper and broadcasting organisation. He told a number of journalists that efforts by him to smash a 'cosy cartel' in the semi-state sector had led to a 'sinister' surveillance operation on his private and commercial life. Lowry used the term 'cosy cartel' at least twice, yet 18 months later, he said under oath, 'It was an infamous phrase that was attributed to me and in fact one that was never used by me ....'

At those same briefings on Wednesday, 9 August 1995, an *Irish Times* journalist, echoing the suspicions of some of Lowry's party colleagues, asked Lowry if he had availed of the 1993 tax amnesty. 'All my tax affairs are in order,' he replied. The task force, 'eleven wise men' drawn from the civil service and State companies, and chaired by an assistant secretary in his department, was set up to review existing controls and draw up recommendations to supplement the guidelines controlling State companies. It was a classic 'be seen to do something, do anything' panic attack by an inexperienced minister in deep political trouble and getting drawn further into the mire.

Lowry went on holiday but stayed in daily contact with his media adviser, Bill O'Herlihy, and a daily sheaf of press cuttings were faxed to him. At the end of August, the anonymous letter writer sent out another batch of correspondence containing low grade gossip and a startling claim: there was no surveillance on Lowry, it had been an invention of the author's. The anonymous correspondent had also changed tack: where the writer appeared to be helping Lowry in earlier letters, the minister was now viciously attacked with scurrilous allegations about his private life, and the latest letters were also circulated to Fianna Fáil.

To add to Lowry's woes, some of the most senior and respected public servants were offended and deeply angry over the minister's claims of corruption in the state-owned companies. Trade unions representing workers in the sector also fired a warning shot at Lowry. 'This reckless undermining of the State companies is not what we expect from a minister who was given these companies in trust,' said the secretary of the Irish Congress of Trade Unions' national worker director group.

With some foreboding the government agreed to a special two and a half hour debate in the Dáil on Tuesday, 10 October to discuss a motion of 'no confidence' in Michael Lowry. The opposition sensed his fear while the media said it was make or break or put-up-or-shut-up time for the minister. His team of political, departmental and media advisers treated it as something of a parliamentary All-Ireland Final, but few of them were confident of their man's ability to match the occasion. Departmental officials spent days briefing him and a financial journalist helped draft the 22-page speech, with an input from both the Labour Party's and Democratic Left's press handlers. The Taoiseach's most senior adviser, a former ambassador to the United States, Sean Donlon, and Democratic Left minister, Pat Rabbitte, also pitched in to help the government cause.

However, more experienced political observers said Michael Lowry needed to put on the performance of his life rather than simply deliver a cleverly-crafted speech. The debate would be televised and nothing was left to chance. He visited a hairdresser in Blackrock, Co. Dublin, earlier in the day; he wore a new shirt and tie. He was nervous and his pale face looked haunted in contrast to his dyed black hair. Lowry spoke in a grave monotone for 50 minutes to a crowded and hushed Dáil chamber. He supplied no new facts about the surveillance, and, he failed to prove that any cosy cartel was getting a lion's share of business in the State companies. He outlined the details of the sale of the CIE property at Horgan's Quay in Cork to developer Owen O'Callaghan's company which had already been in the public domain.

Questioned by the opposition, Lowry said three sets of High Court proceedings were instituted against him and invoked a newly-changed *sub judice* rule to justify his refusal to answer questions outlining the basis for his surveillance allegations. There was even more bad news: the task force he had set up to enquire into how the State companies conducted their affairs delivered its report. It concluded, with commendable understatement, 'The commercial State companies stood up well to scrutiny'.

Lowry's fig leaf of cover was blown away by the report written by the 'eleven wise men' drawn from the elite of the civil service and State companies. The task force found little wrong with practises in the State companies. His own party colleagues in cabinet gathered around in support, but there were concerns that the patience of the left-wing coalition partners might be running out. They needn't have worried about Proinsias De Rossa, the leader of Democratic Left, who declared, 'Mr Lowry is an honest man'. The leader of the Labour Party, Dick Spring, was more circumspect. His sixth sense must have been working overtime: more trouble was just 20 days ahead.

From early afternoon on Thursday, 1 November, journalists in Leinster House were hearing that *Prime Time*, RTÉ's flagship current affairs programme, planned to broadcast a sensational story that evening concerning the surveillance on Michael Lowry. I rang the current affairs office and asked if I could go to their studios that night to do a follow-up story for Friday morning's *Irish Independent*. After a series of phone calls, I was invited to appear on a panel discussion to discuss their filmed report.

Meanwhile, other sources confirmed that *Prime Time* had tracked down the author of the anonymous letters about the surveillance. He was identified as an accountant, Pat Tuffy, a former Fianna Fáil activist in Dublin's South Central constituency. It was nearly six o'clock that evening when I phoned the Institute of Chartered Accountants and asked if a Pat Tuffy was registered with them as a practising accountant. They had already spoken to *Prime Time* and had the details to hand: he was a bankrupt and struck off.

RTÉ's lawyers had already seen and cleared the programme *Prime Time* proposed to broadcast. Another journalist, Emily O'Reilly, was on the panel and neither of us saw the film before it was transmitted. It was compelling viewing. On screen, Pat Tuffy matter-of-factly made the most hair-raising claims: he admitted writing all the anonymous letters and an independent handwriting expert, retained by *Prime Time*, confirmed it; he said he wrote the letters under instruction. He also said he had met the minister at his house, in a Dublin restaurant, and at Punchestown Races.

Off screen, he told *Prime Time* that Lowry had paid him £1,100 to write the letters. Discussing the film on air, Emily O'Reilly and I both said that if Tuffy's story was true, it was the biggest political scandal for decades. Immediately after the programme, Michael Lowry issued a statement saying Pat Tuffy's allegations were a total fabrication. He said he did not know Tuffy and never asked him to write anonymous letters to anyone.

He had never paid Tuffy any money or engaged him for any purpose; never arranged to meet him at Punchestown races or anywhere else. He didn't know where Tuffy lived nor visited him at his house; had never been to the Avalon House café nor ever phoned him there. It was a very comprehensive, and very convincing, denial.

The story I wrote for Saturday's *Irish Independent* began, 'Pat Tuffy is suffering from leukaemia, his wife is tormented by a chronic psychiatric disorder and their only son may be taken from them. He is a self-confessed liar, a forger who is forbidden by law to practise as an accountant and a bankrupt who would do anything for money.' Michael Lowry instituted proceedings against Pat Tuffy, RTÉ and me 'seeking exemplary damages for this most grievous and unwarranted libel'. But the minister still had a problem: Tuffy's anonymous letters were the only evidence Michael Lowry had to substantiate his claims to have been under surveillance from criminals employed by businessmen, angry that he had smashed their cosy cartels and their lucrative business with State companies.

It only took another four days for Michael Lowry to hit the headlines again, but this time they offered the beleaguered minister some respite. Pat Tuffy appeared on RTÉ News the following Monday evening and retracted the outrageous allegations he had made on *Prime Time*. Lowry went on the offensive, saying that anyone tempted to ask him about surveillance would find him willing to defend himself aggressively. Although he was vindicated when Tuffy's bizarre allegations were discredited, Lowry was in no mood for magnanimity.

Another controversy was bubbling away in his communications portfolio: the granting of the country's second mobile phone licence to challenge the State-owned monopoly, Eircell, a division of Telecom Éireann. He had awarded the licence, described as the biggest contract ever awarded by the State to a private company, ESAT Telecom, an Irish-dominated consortium, in the face of formidable international competition. Such a valuable property was certain to attract rumours on a ratio comparable to its potential profits, and the whispering predated Lowry's appointment.

Denis O'Brien, the young chairman of ESAT, knocked a hole in the ceiling of his office while punching the air in celebration when the news that his company had secured the licence was relayed to him. The process of choosing the winner was shrouded in secrecy and some of the most powerful multinational corporations had formed consortia with some of the biggest names in Irish business, to seek the licence. Martin Naughton,

Lochlann Quinn, Dermot Desmond and Declan Ganley were among the locally-based entrepreneurs who togged out for corporate Ireland. While AT&T, Motorola, Deutsche Telecom, Unisource and Southwestern Bell represented the best known of the multinationals.

Eventually, six consortia jostled for preference. Motorola were favourites and ESAT's chances took a severe knock when talks between Deutsche Telecom and Southwestern Bell collapsed, sparking off a rumour that the Irish company was holding out for too large a stake in the consortium. But the Norwegian state phone company, Telenor, saved the day and joined the ESAT consortium. Then the government delayed the closing date for applications by six weeks and fixed the price the winning consortium would be required to pay the government at £15 million. It was known that one multinational was prepared to pay £80m.

As rumours circulated in Dublin and around the international telecommunications industry, Minister Lowry brought forward the announcement of the winner and awarded the licence to ESAT on 25 October 1995. Two years later, long after ESAT's service became available to the public, the controversy was only beginning to fade. The questions were awkward: Was the decision to reduce the cap to £15 million made to facilitate the Irish applicant, ESAT and their Norwegian partners, who would never have been able to match the funds available to the multinationals? On 3 March that year, Minister Lowry said the government had not set the size of the fee to be paid for the licence because 'the level of fee will be determined by the market' although he added, 'There is no cheque book policy with regard to this issue'.

The criteria used to select the winner were also questioned when it became known that the charge to the public for each phone call was only the third most important element: this was particularly puzzling after Mr Lowry declared in March that the main criteria would be '... to ensure that the price of the equipment is lowered, and to ensure that tariffs are lowered'. It was also revealed that Denis O'Brien had attended political functions with Michael Lowry, and donated £5,000 by an untraceable bank draft to Fine Gael.

Above all, the secrecy surrounding the process in awarding the licence raised suspicions, and the involvement of the most accident and rumour-prone minister in the government. After the licence was awarded to ESAT, the United States embassy in Dublin made representations to the Irish government asking for some transparency and explanations of the process. It was unfair to ESAT, who had a formidable team of lobbyists drawn from the two major political parties working on their behalf, and had prepared an artfully-crafted bid for the licence. It also signalled that Michael Lowry attracted controversy and could become a liability for the government he served, although he was still the closest minister in cabinet to the Taoiseach.

A Minister for Transport from a rural background was always going to have a problem winning the confidence of Dubliners dealing with such an ultra-sensitive issue as the future of traffic in the capital city. And those who had followed his career knew the fanfare of metaphorical trumpets which heralded Michael Lowry's proposal for a new light rail transit system, to be called LUAS, was ill-judged. The disruption in the city centre and the destruction of the narrow streets leading to it, was heavily criticised. But when Dr Garret FitzGerald, a former Fine Gael Taoiseach, produced a detailed analysis with a proposal to put the system underground, Lowry did what ministers in trouble do: he commissioned a report to examine Dr FitzGerald's criticism.

However Lowry's report was inherently flawed: it was prepared by the same consultants who had produced the earlier report proposing the overground rail system. The £225 million LUAS project was dependent on EU funding and the EU Commission had imposed a time limit on it. Fighting battles on so many other fronts, Michael Lowry had no stomach for confronting another controversy, especially when he was opposed by such a totem of Fine Gael probity as Dr FitzGerald, and besides, other issues were rapidly consuming the minister.

It was *déjà vu*: leaks to the media of a State company executive's expense account, topped off with tales of fine wines, exotic travel and high living. It was a re-run of the tactics, almost the identical *modus operandi*, used to discredit the CIE chairman, Dermot O'Leary, a year before. You didn't need to be a forensic scientist to identify the distinctive political fingerprints of Michael Lowry. The target was Eddie O'Connor, the chief executive of Bord na Móna, ultimately responsible to the Minister for Transport, Energy and Communications. Appointed in 1987, O'Connor was a high flyer in the State companies, outspoken and outstandingly successful, he was also a radical. Just three months before, he had made a speech advocating the privatisation of Bord na Móna which angered some Labour ministers in the Rainbow Coalition, particularly the Tanaiste, Dick Spring.

Why, it was asked, was Eddie O'Connor singled out? He had been held up as an example of what was expected of chief executives in State companies in the 1990s: progressive, market-orientated, and a passionate advocate of modern management techniques. He had cut 2,000 people from the payroll at Bord na Móna at one fifth of the cost of each ESB redundancy and still enjoyed the support of the trade unions and worker directors. Under O'Connor's regime, the profit increased by £21 million, the workforce had been halved and he had persuaded managers to forego pay increases.

A steady drip of details from his expense account were leaked to the media like a Chinese water torture. He had earned between £150,000 and £200,000 when government guidelines capped the basic salary of State company chief executives at £65,618. O'Connor protested that the former chairman of Bord na Móna, Brendan Halligan, had agreed his pay and expenses package with him when he had been headhunted from the ESB nine years before. A former General Secretary of the Labour Party, Brendan Halligan, defended O'Connor and said he had the authority of the board to make the deal in 1987.

Every Sunday another newspaper carried more details from O'Connor's expenses, and the chairman, Pat Dineen, appointed on the recommendation of his friend, Dick Spring, stoically declined to comment. It was a tiny detail from a story leaked to the *Sunday Independent* on 9 June 1996 that turned the tide for O' Connor. Someone had leaked O'Connor's hotel bill for a stay in Orlando in 1994, but it was mistakenly dated 1995 and corrected by pen. By chance, the hotel bill from Orlando was reproduced in the newspaper. O'Connor's secretary had corrected the printed date with a pen and left a mark on the paper before it was given to the chairman, Pat Dineen.

O'Connor's solicitors wrote to Dineen and told him about the changed date on the hotel bill and how it had been changed just before it was sent to him. How, they wanted to know, had that same receipt, with the changed date, been reproduced in the newspaper? Dineen assured O'Connor and his lawyers that nothing had been leaked by him, or by anybody with his authority. O'Connor wrote to all the board members at Bord na Móna telling them about the 'unique annotation' on the leaked document and warned them of their responsibilities. At the next board meeting, when O'Connor raised the matter of the leaked hotel bill, he was suspended. Pat Dineen contacted the officials at the Department of Transport, Energy and Communications, and they spoke to the Attorney General, and the minister, Michael Lowry. The board members were given an assurance they would be indemnified for any legal costs arising from any litigation prompted by the controversy.

It was the first time Lowry had been publicly identified with the controversy. Public opinion began to swing and O'Connor was now being portrayed in the media as the victim of a political witch hunt. A number of ministers were becoming uneasy, even embarrassed, by the crude undermining of Eddie O'Connor, and other chief executives of State companies, who believed the Bord na Móna chief executive had been treated disgracefully, made their feelings known. The Bord na Móna saga ended after 12 weeks, at a late night cabinet meeting, with the government instructing Michael Lowry to conclude negotiations with O'Connor as soon a possible. A settlement package, including pension rights, payment for the year his contract still had to run, compensation for damage to his reputation caused by media leaks and the settlement of his legal bills, was agreed between departmental negotiators and lawyers acting for O'Connor.

For nearly a year Michael Lowry's writ, a personal memento of what somebody called 'Tuffy's Circus', hung over me. In an exchange of letters with Lowry's solicitors, I let them know I would not allow their client, a government minister, to intimidate me personally or professionally. Sources close to the minister leaked stories to the media saying RTÉ had offered to settle the defamation action for £250,000. Concerned at the prospect of a prohibitively expensive and long drawn out legal battle, and anxious not to be isolated, I contacted Bob Collins, now the Director General of RTÉ and he assured me no settlement was imminent.

After an exchange of letters with my solicitor, RTÉ's legal department agreed to idemnify me against any legal costs or a future settlement of the case. At least part of Lowry's reasoning for taking the legal action, was to make me aware of the possible consequences of criticising him in the future, and RTÉ's undertaking made it much easier to continue reporting on the most controversial minister in the government.

Chapter Eleven

Like civil war, siblings' squabbles are less inhibited and more vicious than disputes between strangers. When relatives fall out, the hurt is greater, the wounds are deeper and they take longer to heal. Less privileged families may disagree over who gets what piece of furniture after the death of a parent, but the very rich are different. They have the means to hire lawyers as proxy warriors and instruct them to be as ruthless and cruel as their professional ethics permit. It allows enough latitude to license torment in legal battles between kith and kin. But it is too easy to blame the lawyers for the malice of their clients: ultimate responsibility lies with the people who instruct them and pay the bills. Lawyers with a reputation for inflicting the most pain on their clients' opponents are in heavy demand and it is reflected in the fees they charge. Rich people with a legal problem never ask their friends if they can recommend a cheap, mild-mannered lawyer.

In 1993, the inner tensions of the Dunne family burst out of the privacy of the boardroom and into open court. After Ben Dunne was stripped of all executive functions on 5 July, writs flew and the finest silks in the land were recruited as infantry when the family went to war. If they were street traders arguing in the District Court, a judge might have told them to sort out their differences in private. But they were in the High Court, and while less sophisticated folk might have thought there were just two parties in dispute, five teams of the most able and expensive lawyers in the land togged out for the confrontation. No one should have been surprised. The prize was control of 66 stores, employing 6,000 people, turning over almost a billion pounds a year and making a profit of a million pounds a week.

But while their grand corporate arguments were to be teased out before a judge, mundane details of everyday life in the board room were more revealing about inter-sibling relations. Ben accused his siblings of 'ill-will and malice' towards him; the next day his sister Margaret said his behaviour was 'intolerable'. The board had taken away Ben's office keys; Ben had stubbed out his cigarette in Margaret's glass of mineral water.

The rest of the Dunnes, particularly Margaret, believed Ben's solicitor, Noel Smyth, had too powerful an influence over their brother and company policy. She saw Smyth as a cuckoo in the Dunnes' gilded nest. It appalled her when Noel Smyth was appointed her younger brother's legal guardian by a court in Orlando and both Frank Dunne and Margaret were unhappy with Smyth's role in Dunnes Stores' property dealings.

Between them, Dunnes Stores and Quinnsworth sold 48 per cent of all the food bought in the Republic. Consequently, Dunnes had enormous clout dealing with the developers of shopping centres. Frank Dunne, who had been in charge of the property portfolio, had his own personal problems and had not taken such an active interest in the company before the split with Ben. Noel Smyth was something of an expert in property and had always enjoyed Ben's full confidence, but after he was fired, Dunnes Stores took legal action against Smyth and he counter-sued them.

Ben had been taunting Margaret Heffernan, telling her he had made payments of £1 million to Charles Haughey. 'You can look all you like, but you'll never find them', he teased. She loathed Haughey because of the incident in 1968 when he had humiliated her father at the trade fair in New York. Margaret found it difficult to believe Ben, but decided to visit Haughey to check it out in July or early August in 1993. She met Haughey alone at Abbeville and asked him if her brother had given him £1.1 million. Haughey said he couldn't be responsible for what her brother said. She pressed him but he avoided answering and steered the conversation to Ben's apparent instability.

She visited Des Traynor at his office and said to him that her brother Bernard claimed to have given Haughey a million pounds. Traynor said he knew absolutely nothing about it. In November, shortly before the trust court hearing, she visited Haughey again in Abbeville. This time she knew from a pleading made by Ben in his High Court action to break the family trust that her brother had paid Haughey £1.1 million. But she never mentioned the money because she believed that anything she said to Haughey would be relayed back to Ben. It was the former Taoiseach who instigated the meeting, he tried to impress on her the importance of reaching a settlement with Ben. Haughey said that the Dunnes should not be going into court and fighting in public. In November 1994, solicitors for Dunnes Stores had formally written to Haughey asking him to return their £1.1 million.

The mutual enmity between Margaret Heffernan and Noel Smyth led to an exchange of writs. Smyth was seeking £476,000 in unpaid legal fees for work his firm of solicitors did on Ben Dunne's instructions when he was chairman. Dunnes Stores claimed damages from Smyth for deceit, misrepresentation, abuse of authority, breach of duty and negligence, plus the return of a £500,000 deposit paid for a site in north Dublin. It was really only a preliminary bout before the main attraction: Ben's legal action to break the family trust.

It wasn't just the Dunnes who distrusted and disliked Noel Smyth, other lawyers and former clients spoke ill of him too, but he was never accused of being stupid. He was, and is, totally focused on his work: and has no known bad habits. Curiously, some of his detractors cite his daily Mass-going and religiosity as character defects. A family man with few outside interests beyond work, one of his hobbies is classic cars. Smyth told a friend that his children will be, but he never saw himself as a part of the Establishment.

The son of a professional golfer, his family had lived in various parts of the country when he was growing up. He qualified as a solicitor following graduation from UCD in 1973 and started his own firm in 1981 after leaving a partnership in another Dublin firm. While his first love has always been the law, he has been staggeringly successful in his business and property dealings. Now in his mid-forties, he is worth an estimated £20 million. One of his biggest financial coups took place in 1987 when he was part of the team put together by financier Paschal Taggart which bought the H. Williams supermarket chain for £14 million. He had 13 per cent of the company and they sold on the stores to Quinnsworth, Dunnes Stores and Musgraves within weeks, making a handsome profit.

The inquiry into the purchase of the Johnston, Mooney and O'Brien site in Ballsbridge and its sale to Telecom, revealed that Smyth had been brought into one of the complicated series of transactions to arrange a tax-efficient financial package for Dermot Desmond, who ran NCB stockbrokers at that time. Pat Doherty, a property developer, said at the Telecom enquiry that Smyth was the sort of solicitor 'to whom you went for advice only to come away with a business partner'. Smyth's role in the affair was established by the Inspector John Glackin as entirely legitimate. Rivals have grudgingly acknowledged his formidable intelligence and skills as a business and tax lawyer.

In 1993 Smyth bought out Ben Dunne's share in the property company Dunloe House and paid £700,000 for the 75 per cent stake. Their involvement in the publicly-quoted company which had the potential to launch serious competition to Dunnes Stores, had further angered the family.

In a rare interview in 1995, he told the financial journalist Des Crowley about his plans to break into the movie business with Don Tidey, the supermarket executive who was kidnapped in 1983. 'I'm involved with Don Tidey in setting up a 13-part film on the life of Jesus Christ for a cost of $7m using Section 35 finance and equity supplied by myself and Don Tidey.' The business proposition was a neat summary of all of Noel Smyth's known specialist interests: a previously-kidnapped supermarket tycoon, religion and a tax incentive.

He didn't confine his good counsel to the business community. In February 1996 Noel Smyth turned up as an adviser to the Bishop of Ferns, Dr Brendan Comiskey, when he returned to Ireland after treatment for alcoholism and a series of controversies in his diocese.

As the Dunne family headed toward a potentially ruinous confrontation, sources close to Ben explained his position: 'They would have liked to say to Ben, "Look, you're gone now. We don't mind paying you £1.5 million a year the same as us, and we'll pay you all the other bonuses that we get. You make your own arrangements, but stay away from Stephen's Street".'

Still stung by Ben's taunts of giving away £1 million to Haughey and his threat to bring down the family trust, Dunnes Stores commissioned independent auditors, Price Waterhouse, to investigate payments made by Ben when he was chairman. Price Waterhouse's report would be the backbone of the Dunne trust's defence against Ben's action. In her affidavit, Margaret Heffernan said Ben's behaviour after his appointment as chairman became 'increasingly erratic and irresponsible' and criticised his 'buying spree' in Britain and his trip to Singapore with Noel Smyth to purchase cheap clothing. She said sometimes the deals he made were 'cash' payments without negotiating any normal credit terms and he didn't have board approval to spend £20 million. 'These purchases have apparently been negotiated in a hotel in Singapore. They involved serious and damaging commitments for the company and I have continued to endeavour to get these contracts cancelled,' said Margaret.

Ben Dunne lodged his claim in the High Court on 22 September 1994 where he alleged that the trust 'was at all times a sham' and that it was never intended 'to be a discretionary trust.' He claimed some of the directors instructed him to pay money into overseas banks, and into accounts they held in fictitious names, and that Margaret and Therese had been made payments through fictitious names.

The trust was set up in 1964 and stipulated that the siblings would be entitled to their share of the assets after 21 years. However in March 1985 when it was due to be broken up, they faced a £40 million tax bill and decided to postpone the vesting of the trust. Subsequently a deed of appointment was granted to the four trustees: Noel Fox, Frank Bowen, Bernard Uniacke and Edward Montgomery. Under the terms of the deed appointment, the trustees had the power to distribute the assets of the trust at any time they chose. Failing that, the assets couldn't be distributed until after the death of Margaret, Frank, Therese, Ben and Anne, the sister who is in residential care. Ben claimed that some family members ignored the conditions of the trust and used the assets as they wished, which made the trust 'a sham'.

Smyth took the role of Field Marshall in Ben's battle against the family trust. Both Smyth and Ben Dunne came under enormous pressure from some of the most powerful people in the country to settle the dispute amicably. Charles Haughey spoke to, and met, Smyth regularly in 1993 and 1994 to discuss the Dunne family's dispute. Others approached Smyth and said if he backed off, the family would settle with Ben. He was told that if he lost the case, the Dunnes have so much clout, banks wouldn't deal with him. It didn't deter Smyth, if anything, it stiffened his resolve: if people got hurt in the cross fire, that's too bad. Casualties were inevitable when the stakes were so high. Smyth lined up three of the leading senior counsel in the country to represent Ben Dunne in the trust action: Dermot Gleeson, Paul Gallagher and Peter Kelly. There were four top firms of solicitors, each with a team of leading counsel representing the various Dunnes' interests.

Smyth told his colleagues that he wanted to win for several reasons. First, it was probably the biggest case he was ever likely to handle; second, he was very fond of Ben. He told a friend, 'He drives me fucking mad at times, but I genuinely like him. And a terrible injustice was being done to him.' Smyth said he didn't want emotion to become involved. The way he saw it, Gleeson, Gallagher and Kelly are top professionals, and you can only work with them providing you don't let emotion get involved and you don't let personalities get involved. Ben was kept away from most of the meetings until a decision had to be made. None of the other solicitors in his office were involved, Smyth handled the case himself.

Dunnes assumed that Ben Dunne and Noel Smyth would get tired, intimidated or they would run out of resources fighting four other legal teams. The Price Waterhouse Report was the Dunnes' ace card. Smyth took an action claiming that Price Waterhouse were not independent. Through discovery, they found out that Price Waterhouse had asked Frank Dunne what exactly did he want investigated and where should they concentrate their efforts. Smyth argued that the Price Waterhouse investigation wasn't independent and was specifically prepared for litigation, therefore it was jaundiced. It seriously undermined Dunnes Stores' case against Ben Dunne.

After the case was resolved, Smyth's legal tactics became clear. As far as he was concerned, anybody going into a legal or business war should be very happy with somebody like him on their side, and the enemy could only expect pain. There were no rules because all the rules had been taken off the table. Smyth spent a lot of time building a case to destroy the trust. Ben Dunne and Smyth went to London with accountants to negotiate with Slaughter and May the merchant bankers, to raise capital to bid for his siblings' shares; Ben offered them £400 million. But, more importantly, making the bid put a value of £80 million on Ben's shares. Somewhat disingenuously, Smyth maintained that the family were attacking Ben personally but that he was just attacking the trust.

On the Sunday night, two days before the case was due to start in November 1994, counsel for Dunnes Stores, Nial Fennelly, rang Ben Dunne's counsel, Dermot Gleeson at midnight. They were prepared to talk. On Monday, Smyth started moving his dozens of boxes of files to the courts. On Tuesday morning in the Four Courts, Mr Justice Murphy was in Court Number Four and his first words were to ask if anyone objected to him hearing the case as he had acted for Frank Dunne when he was a barrister. There were no objections. Then they asked for an adjournment and the case was settled. Ben received an estimated £125 million, which was to be paid over three years, the last tranche, more than £30 million, was paid in December 1996. Ben Dunne's legal bills were reported to be between £5 million and £7 million.

Ben Dunne's claim that the trust was a sham was bound to attract the interest of the Revenue Commissioners. It is understood that Ben Dunne's tax bill for the settlement, estimated at around £30 million, was the largest ever tendered by any individual in the history of the State.

Ben Dunne had joined his own roll-call of Dunnes Stores' fallen heroes. Less than a year before, two financial controllers, Michael Irwin and Niall Walsh were dismissed in October 1993. This was followed by the walkout of four senior executives, head of overhead controls, Tony Sheehan, drapery administrator, Senan McGonigle, grocery accounts manager, Joe Cummins and drapery accounts manager, Dave O'Connor. The resignations were a protest at the dismissal of their colleagues. Margaret Heffernan wanted to erase all of Ben's influence and rid the company of anyone who was friendly to her younger brother. Like so many before him who didn't have a financial trampoline to rebound from redundancy, he ranked idleness close to heresy. More than almost anyone, Ben Dunne's identity was defined by what he did, more than who he was. Besides an inherited and deeply ingrained work ethic, his know-how had quadrupled his father's business to a billion-pound retailing empire.

Golf, always a passion, became something of an obsession when he had so much free time. A body clock set through more than 30 years to activate around 6.30 a.m., couldn't easily be reprogrammed to allow long lie-ins and early nights when he was in semi-retirement. From the early 1990s, Ben had an interest in the fine arts. His mentor, Noel Smyth, had started buying paintings in 1969, when he purchased a Brian Maguire. Ben, who never does anything in half-measures, spent more and more time in galleries after he left the supermarket business. It took some time for Dunne and Smyth to figure out they were bidding against each other for pictures: it was a lop-sided contest, and Ben's greater resources dictated the outcome. Smyth had more experience but Dunne had more money. They decided to form a partnership to buy Irish paintings.

In February 1995, Dunne purchased his favourite painting, Sir John Lavery's *Requiem Of A Mass For Michael Collins*, from Alan Hobard, a London dealer for 'a hefty six figure sum.' A couple of months later, he used a dealer to buy Jack Yeats' *Singing the Dark Rosaleen at Croke Park* at Sotheby's in London for £450,000. Painted in 1921, critic Hilary Pyle described the painting as, 'one of the masterpieces of Yeats' early style. A rare example of a political subject painted by Yeats in a characteristically oblique way.' At the time, Ben joked about his barring from Dunnes Stores and the sour relations with his family, 'They can keep me out of the stores, but they can't keep me out of the paint shops.' At one time, an old master in Ben Dunne's house would have been a photograph of an ageing golfer in a green jacket. But now Lavery's *Requiem* has pride of place, and Yeats' *Dark Rosaleen* is also on display in his Castleknock home. After a couple of years, Smyth and Dunne dissolved the partnership when they both wanted to hang the same paintings in their homes.

His plans for a chain of indoor and outdoor health and fitness centres were well advanced when another personal tragedy further complicated the corporate litigation and sibling enmity. Therese Dunne, the youngest in the family and known to them as Theresa, died unexpectedly in September 1995. Ben and Therese had been very close as children. A bond grew between the youngest two when they stayed at home in Cork while the rest of the family holidayed abroad. She never married and her talent as a buyer of children's clothes had contributed enormously to the success of Dunnes Stores in recent years. Like her older sister Margaret, a 52-week sun tan made her something of a terracotta warrior, tough as old boots in business, but personally generous.

Therese, it was said, never needed lessons in self-assertion. Making hard choices came as easy to her as disciplining querulous staff. In a family where alcohol had taken an horrendous toll over three generations, she left £6 million in her will to research into alcoholism. Although her withdrawal of support from Ben had led to his sacking as chairman two years before, Therese's death was deeply unsettling for him so soon after his humbling by Margaret. Her estate was valued at £22 million, but that did not include her share of the trust, worth £125 million, which she left to Margaret. Ben began a legal action to contest the will, reckoning that Therese's shares would be distributed among the remaining shareholders enriching them by £41.7 million each.

Dunnes Stores had discovered from the Price Waterhouse Report that they had paid £395,000 for the refurbishment and extension to Michael Lowry's house in Tipperary. Although his company, Streamline, continued to do refrigeration work for the company, Margaret Heffernan was said to be angry that her younger brother had made such a sweetheart deal with Lowry. There were also rumours that Ben might have been angry that Michael Lowry seemed closer to Dunnes Stores than himself. Caught in an irrational tug of loyalties between such conflicting and irresistible forces, Lowry must have wondered what was coming next.

Chapter Twelve

It was half past eleven on a Thursday night in early October 1996 when I picked up the phone at home; I was tired and the caller was nervous. He had rung twice before, he said, but didn't leave a message on the answering machine. More of an acquaintance than a friend, I wondered where he had got my ex-directory home telephone number as we went through a ritual foreplay of polite small talk before getting down to business. He had been following my reporting about Michael Lowry in the columns of the *Irish Independent* with interest, would I meet him to discuss it further?

Too much of my adult life has been spent in anonymous pubs meeting contacts with stories to tell, and most of these clandestine assignations have been with somebody wanting to get even with someone they don't like. Rarely do any of these avenging angels have any evidence to support their scurrilous allegations which means that dutiful reporters waste countless hours as surrogate psychologists for busy-bodies and cranks. Still, curiosity and hope usually prevail over grim experience.

I agreed to meet my contact the next afternoon, in a suitably anonymous public building. He was sweating and agitated, insisted that I never identify him in any circumstances and said we shouldn't be seen together again. I agreed and he got down to business. Did I know that Dunnes Stores had paid for the refurbishment and extension of Michael Lowry's home in Tipperary? No, I said, but even if they did, his company worked for Dunnes Stores and there might well be an innocent explanation. My informant said Ben Dunne had made his financial arrangement privately with Lowry, unknown to Dunnes Stores, and that the cost of the extension and refurbishment of Lowry's house had been charged to a branch of Dunnes Stores in Dublin. More than £200,000 was involved, he said, and the work on Lowry's house had been done by Dunnes Stores' builder and architect. Although my informant had no connection with Dunnes Stores, Ben Dunne or Michael Lowry, I was convinced he had access to the truth. I told him the story couldn't be published without overwhelming proof and sufficient documentary evidence to satisfy myself, the editor of the *Irish Independent* and the paper's lawyers.

He said he would see what he could do and promised to phone me at home. At our next meeting, my contact showed me a photocopy of an Ulster Bank cheque for £76,674.16, dated 24 February 1993, signed personally by Ben Dunne and payable to the builders, Faxhill Homes. He also showed me a photocopy of an invoice from Faxhill Homes, dated 25 February 1993, for the same amount of money referring to work done at the Ilac centre branch of Dunnes Stores. How, I asked, was the invoice dated for a day after the cheque was written? He didn't know, but explained to me the cheque for £76,674.16 was the final instalment of three payments, totalling £207,674, for work done on Lowry's house.

The documents were convincing but there was still not enough proof to approach Lowry or publish the story. I asked my informant if the information had come to light when Dunnes Stores had commissioned an internal report from independent auditors when Ben Dunne was involved in a legal action to break up the Dunnes family trust. He shrugged off the question, but I asked him to get me a copy of the report. My informant was frustrated and suspicious of my continual questions and demands for documentation. He agreed to meet again and he showed me photocopies of what I was convinced were pages taken from the auditor's report. I asked if I could have a copy of the documents, but he couldn't allow them out of his possession. Unless I could get copies of the documents, the story couldn't be published. Ten minutes of my explaining the level of proof required to satisfy the libel lawyers, convinced him of my seriousness and frustration. He couldn't promise to get me copies of the documents, but he would do his damnedest. The next question was: Would the *Irish Independent* publish it if I did get a copy of the documents?

Vincent Doyle sat in the editor's office on the first floor of Independent House, his television, as always, tuned to Sky News, with all of that morning's British and Irish newspapers neatly folded on the conference table in front of his desk. He looked up and listened, without interruption, to the tale of Lowry, his home improvements and Dunnes Stores. 'Great story if you can stand it up', he said.

A week later I went to Los Angeles to cover the opening of Riverdance in Hollywood and the civil action against OJ Simpson in Santa Monica. Returning to my hotel one evening, I received a message from Dublin that my informant was urgently trying to contact me. I flew home the following Wednesday for the launch of the book I had written on

Riverdance. I called my informant when I arrived in Dublin on Thursday morning, but he was very uneasy talking on the telephone. The earliest he could see me was the next afternoon, a couple of hours before the book launch.

Like many people, his knowledge of investigative journalism seemed to have been learned from the film, *All The President's Men*. He insisted we meet in the car park of a pub in Clontarf, on the north side of Dublin. Nervous the first time we met, by now my informant was paranoid as he sat into the front seat of my car and carefully took the photocopies out of his briefcase as if they were nuclear secrets. There were copies of the cheque, copies of invoices and copies of the architect's certificate which showed the total value of the work completed at the Ilac centre, Dublin, which amounted to £207,819.73 and authorised the final payment of £76,674.16 to Faxhill Homes.

Jet-lagged and slightly disorientated, I thought of the bloody glove in the OJ Simpson trial when I read the covering letter from the architect to Dunnes Stores. It said the payment was, in fact, for alterations and additions to Michael Lowry's house in Holycross, Co. Tipperary. A photocopy of a page from the internal report for Dunnes Stores, prepared by auditors, Price Waterhouse, seemed to me to be conclusive proof. It read, 'Architect's certificate and invoice from Faxhill Homes indicate that this payment is in respect of work done at Dunnes Stores. However, the cover letter from Peter Stevens & Associates, Architects, indicates that the payment is in respect of work at Glenreigh, Holycross for Mr M. Lowry. The amount certified to the date of this payment was £207,820. We understand Mr M Lowry is connected with Streamline Enterprises Ltd, a company which supplies refrigeration services to Dunnes Stores.' When he was leaving, my informant seemed strangely elated, wished me good luck and said he didn't want to see or talk to me again for a long time.

Vincent Doyle studied the documents. 'Are you sure you're not being set up?' was his instinctive reaction. 'People can turn out perfect forgeries with a modern word processor and the latest photocopying machines,' he said. I told him my informant wouldn't knowingly do that; he said my contact's motive was not as important as the authenticity of the documents.

Gerard Fanning, the *Independent's* solicitor, was surprised when he saw the documents supporting the story: 'if the photocopies are of the original documents, the story can be published', he said authoritatively. His advice was that Lowry should be given every opportunity to know what the *Irish Independent* intended to publish and wait for his reaction. If the information was wrong, it was in the minister's interest to let us know. By this time, I had checked with other sources familiar with Lowry and Dunnes Stores and they believed that the documents were almost certainly part of the infamous Price Waterhouse Report. The documents had been seen by at least a dozen lawyers, one source said, they were on file in a number of lawyers' offices and the auditors' offices for a couple of years. 'As time passes, people get careless,' he added. My informant was neither a lawyer nor an accountant.

On the morning of 28 November, I wrote out a list of a dozen questions asking Michael Lowry: who had paid for the refurbishment and extension of his house? Was it Dunnes Stores? Did he know the £208,000 cost was charged to a Dunnes Stores branch in the Ilac Centre in Dublin? I read the questions out carefully to a woman in the press office at the Department of Transport, Energy and Communications. I asked for a reply from the minister by that afternoon as we intended publishing a story in the next day's *Irish Independent*.

Around noon, I rang Richard Moore, the departmental press officer, on his mobile phone in Brussels and he assured me the questions had been given to the minister. Later that afternoon, when Moore was no longer taking calls, it became apparent the minister was not going to respond. It took maybe 50 minutes to write the story. I filed it to the *Irish Independent* and it was then relayed to the solicitor. The only part of the text removed by the lawyers before it was cleared for publication was Lowry's salary. The lawyers reckoned it was provocative to write that the minister's annual salary was £69,758 in the same story where Dunnes Stores had allegedly paid £208,000 for an extension to his house.

Michael Lowry had flown out to Brussels late in the afternoon of 27 November to prepare for a meeting of the EU Ministers of Communications. 'Porn on the internet' was just one item on a long agenda for the next day's meeting and Lowry stayed in conference with his officials for nearly five hours. It was around 11 p.m. when he concluded the meeting and left to join his press officer, Richard Moore, who was waiting in Kitty O'Shea's pub with three journalists from Tipperary. The Irish government had been widely praised for its quiet efficiency in handling the EU Presidency and like other ministers, Lowry had spent a lot of time away from his constituency.

Anne O'Grady of the *Tipperary Star*, Colm Kinsella of the *Nenagh Guardian* and a reporter from the local independent radio station, John Keating, had been flown out at Lowry's personal expense, to tell the folks back home how the local hero was cutting the mustard with the big boys in Brussels. Lowry had a seven o'clock start the next morning but stayed nearly an hour chatting to the journalists in the pub before leaving them with Moore and heading off to his hotel. Lowry's grounding in GAA and county council politics was an ideal training ground for chairing a meeting of EU ministers. He had a healthy disregard for bureaucracy and wouldn't tolerate jargon from officials who were impressed when he had often figured out other ministers' positions before they knew themselves. Richard Moore was with his three journalist charges when he took a call on his mobile phone from the department around 11 o'clock the next morning. A colleague in the press office in Dublin told him Sam Smyth of the *Irish Independent* had submitted a list of questions for answer by the minister. Moore asked his colleague to fax them to him at the Irish delegation's office.

The press officer read the list of detailed questions asking about the extension and refurbishment of Lowry's home and who paid for them, and passed them on to Lowry's private secretary, Pat O'Connor. She gave them to the minister. He looked at them, said nothing and continued to chair the meeting. The minister's special advisor on EU affairs, Mark Kennelly, took a call from Tipperary on his mobile phone outside the meeting. He was told that Catherine Lowry, the minister's wife, was very distressed. A light aircraft was flying low and making passes over the house in Holycross. A journalist of 17 years experience before he became a press officer, Moore guessed correctly that it was a photographer from the *Irish Independent* taking aerial photographs.

Unlike the other ministers who can excuse themselves and take a break, the chairman couldn't leave the meeting. They didn't break for lunch that day and Lowry ate while wearing headphones to hear the translation of the other ministers' comments. All afternoon, Moore was outside trying to keep the three journalists happy while taking a stream of calls, many of them from the *Irish Independent*, seeking a response to their questions. Around five o'clock, he switched off his phone. The meeting didn't end until half past six and Moore was surprised when Lowry took the chair at the press conference half an hour later. When he had finished answering questions, he turned to Moore and asked him to look after the journalists from Tipperary and headed to Brussels airport.

When Lowry hadn't responded to the questions, the editor of the *Irish Independent*, Vincent Doyle, decided to splash the story on page one. It was around half past nine that evening when the minister's aircraft touched down in Dublin. He had been in contact with the Taoiseach to warn him of the story due to be published the next day and then contacted the leaders of the other two government parties, Dick Spring and Proinsias De Rossa. Lowry got an early edition of the newspaper around one o'clock and a copy of the story was faxed from the department to Richard Moore in Brussels. Lowry had other, more personal difficulties too. An aunt to whom he was particularly close, his godmother, had died and he was expected to join his family in Tipperary. The embattled minister remained silent and spent most of the Friday shuttling between his lawyer's and accountant's offices.

It was noon before Richard Moore arrived back at his office in Dublin and by then the press office in the Department of Transport, Energy and Communications was inundated with queries and requests for interviews with the minister. Moore issued a holding statement saying the minister was meeting with his advisers, but reporters and photographers were already crowded around the door and in the reception area of the department's offices on Kildare Street. As the afternoon wore on, Moore spoke to Lowry and advised him that he couldn't maintain the silence for much longer and whatever about the journalists, the other two parties in government were also demanding an explanation. The media were becoming increasingly impatient and Moore urged Lowry to say something. He had to drive to Tipperary that evening and arranged to speak to RTÉ's special correspondent, Charlie Bird, at the Green Isle Hotel which was on his route home. Charlie Bird arranged a rendezvous with technicians and a mobile satellite van at the hotel to record an interview with the minister for the *Six One News*.

Earlier that afternoon, the Taoiseach was shaken, but stirred himself sufficiently to make a few curious pronouncements. Although he had been aware of the story before it was published, Bruton tried to buy time. He said he had only given the story in that morning's *Irish Independent* 'a cursory glance'. Then he said that the private business dealings of a TD were in 'a different category' than those after an appointment to cabinet. Michael McDowell, chairman of the Progressive Democrats, was incredulous. 'Are we really to believe that John Bruton thought it acceptable for his party chairman and a prominent front bench public representative to have his home massively refurbished at the expense of a large commercial company under any circumstances? He first claimed to have only given the newspaper story only a cursory inspection. That was a monstrous thing to say. His implication, presumably, was that he had more important things to do than read a fairly short and simply written front page story carefully. I simply don't believe that he had not taken the two or three minutes needed to read the story very carefully. If he didn't, he shouldn't be Taoiseach. The story concerned his government and one of of his closest political associates. If true, the story was very serious news. But John Bruton publicly maintained that he had only read it cursorily.'

Richard Moore travelled in Charlie Bird's car to the hotel, but they were followed by photographers and another reporter, Mark Costigan, from a Dublin radio station, FM 104. Later, other cabinet ministers said they knew Lowry was finished when they saw him interviewed on television. He looked like a rabbit caught in the headlights of a car, according to one, and he was particularly unconvincing when he claimed to be the victim of a vendetta by one journalist. The minister did his best to look determined, even defiant: he wouldn't be hounded out of public life. But his pale, drawn face and the dread and fear in his eyes contradicted his bullish statement. When he had finished the interview, Lowry told the journalists that another politician had received £1 million from Ben Dunne.

As the night wore on, Lowry's credibility was in free fall. An adviser to Dick Spring said the Labour Party would be looking for a full explanation of Lowry's arrangement with Dunnes Stores. They were concerned about the tax implications and said a tax clearance certificate wouldn't be enough to satisfy them.

In Lowry's home village of Holycross, the mood was 'deeply sombre', wrote Noel Smith in the *Irish Independent*. One villager described his resignation as 'a thunderbolt out of the sky.' His house had been unoccupied for much of the day, the telephone wasn't answered and a local publican, Ned Ryan of Newport, described Mr Lowry as a 'tremendous minister' and said he had helped everyone, 'irrespective of politics, he was a real gentleman and his work for the constituency was wonderful'.

From early on Saturday morning there was intense speculation about Michael Lowry's future, but as the day wore on the continuing silence from Government Buildings made his resignation inevitable. No plausible explanation had been offered to the other party leaders in government or the Taoiseach. A bone-chilling wind whipped around the posse of reporters and press photographers gathered at the gates of Government Buildings, looking like human hand grenades in their panel-stitched quilted coats.

John Bruton had been meeting officials and the Attorney General, Dermot Gleeson, in his office all day. Gleeson had been placed in a difficult situation professionally. He had acted for Ben Dunne in his action against the Dunne family trust. Like the other lawyers in the case, he must have seen the Price Waterhouse Report which contained the details of Lowry's house extension and who paid for it. He would almost certainly have known about Ben Dunne's million pound payment to Haughey. One of the country's most able barristers and a close friend of Bruton's, he had allowed his house in Dublin to be used for the negotiations for the formation of the Rainbow Coalition government two years before. He was also friendly with Lowry, but his professional ethics forbade him telling anyone, including the Taoiseach, about any of the details in the Dunne trust case.

Michael Lowry sat in the front passenger seat and two officials with a bale of files were in the back of the ministerial Mercedes when it pulled up at the gates of Government Buildings. It was just after half-past three and photographers swooped on the windscreen like locusts. No one opened the gates. The minister looked dazed but forced a smile and gave a thumbs up, just as politicians in trouble have done through the ages. The gates still didn't open. Photographers stretched themselves across the bonnet to get better shots and reporters shouted questions through the window. Lowry's grin was fixed, he looked anxiously at his garda driver then reached across and leaned on the car horn. The electronically-controlled gates parted slowly like the Red Sea and a taxi driver passing down Merrion Street shouted, 'Dunnes Stores better value'.

More television crews, reporters and photographers joined the vigil at the gates. At 6.25 p.m., Richard Moore handed out copies of the resignation statement; five minutes later the Taoiseach stood beside Michael Lowry who still wore that grim grin. 'Yes indeed. I'll pose with my friend. Best friend. Friends for life,' said Lowry while the Taoiseach tried valiantly to smile, although he looked tense and apprehensive. The government press secretary was asked if Mr Lowry would answer questions. 'The man's gone now. He'll choose when he talks to you,' said Shane Kenny.

The church bells for seven o'clock Mass were ringing as Michael Lowry TD, stripped of power, walked down the spectacular staircase in Government Buildings to face the press. His eyes were brimming and he was extremely nervous, but he kept his composure. He put his trembling hands in his pockets and asked journalists to listen to what he had to say. He asked for time and space for him and his family. 'I've played three rounds of golf in the last four years. I might even get good at it this time,' he said, and drove off to his office to make some calls. It must have seemed a symbolic last act: on the day he resigned, ESAT switched on its phone network for the first time.

From Saturday, the £1,000 a week spin doctors began making calls and Sunday's papers were full of 'sources close to Mr Lowry' stories saying the former minister had the use of 'credit facilities' from Dunnes Stores, which were simply an advance on a bonus he was due from the company. He had done nothing wrong and was the victim of a vindictive media campaign.

Friends, neighbours and constituents had started to assemble at the Anner hotel in Thurles at mid-afternoon on Sunday, ignoring the driving rain and biting wind. They were showing solidarity with their man, and they were angry: he was the victim of a media conspiracy. It was a tragedy, a decent man brought down. Michael Lowry arrived quietly, alone, and almost unnoticed as he parked his car in front of the hotel. He was 24 hours from a life where there was an adviser at each elbow and an official driver at the wheel. When the crowd recognised him on the steps of the hotel, he was mobbed, showered with kisses and winded by bear hugs. 'It seemed more of a triumphant send-off than a homecoming for a humbled hero,' wrote Brian McDonald in Monday's *Irish Independent*. Michael Lowry said he was overwhelmed, that he was mentally and physically shattered. He said he would 'absolutely not be forced out of public life', that he would overcome 'this set back' and work his way back to where he had been. Asked about opposition calls for an investigation of his affairs by the Revenue Commissioners, he said, 'I never had a problem with the Revenue, I don't have now and I will not have it in the future.'

While some reporters were writing Lowry's political obituaries, others were trying to stand up a more sensational story which Lowry had hinted at the night before he resigned: the one about the other politician, £1 million and Ben Dunne. However, the disgraced former minister's press handlers now added the name guaranteed to drive the media into a feeding frenzy: Charles Haughey.

GRIFFITH COLLEGE CORK
Cove Street,
Sullivan's Quay, Cork
Tel. +353 - 21 - 450 7027
Fax. +353 - 21 - 4507659
www.gcc.ie

Chapter Thirteen

Mr You Know Who could have been a cartoon germ in an advertisement for a new brand of miracle bathroom cleaner. The name kept popping up like a cryptic clue in a media whodunnit after the resignation of the 'Mr Clean' of Irish politics, Michael Lowry. The pseudonym was usually followed by a 'a former senior Fianna Fáil minister who is alleged to have received £1.1 million from Dunnes Stores.' Charles Haughey was the name 'sources close to Michael Lowry' were dropping to journalists, but fearful of the draconian defamation laws, no newspaper would publish the former Taoiseach's name. Michael Wolsey, the deputy editor of the *Irish Independent*, dreamed up *Mr You Know Who* as a tease for the readers and a libel-proof shorthand title for Mr H. *Phoenix* magazine was first to name Haughey on 6 December 1996. But it was only after *Irish Times* Finance Editor, Cliff Taylor, reported that Charles Haughey had received £1 million from Dunnes Stores, that the shocking truth became common knowledge.

The introduction of Haughey also diverted attention from the hapless Michael Lowry who insisted he had done no wrong and wanted time to consult his accountants and lawyers. His media advisers were very busy too: they said the £208,000 Dunnes Stores paid to refurbish and extend his house was an advance on a bonus and that he had the use of 'credit facilities' from the company. Lowry said he would make a personal statement to the Dáil which would explain his complex relationship with Dunnes Stores. He chose the last sitting before Christmas, late in the afternoon of Thursday, 19 December, to deliver the 19-page statement.

Public speaking was never Michael Lowry's forte and now he had to convince his 165 fellow TDs of his fitness to serve alongside them in the Dáil. It was ironic. Since he had been appointed a government minister two years before, he had been conducting a one man crusade against 'cosy cartels' and corruption in Irish business and public life. Lowry wanted to 'set the record straight' about his relationship with Dunnes Stores and maintained he had discharged his responsibilities properly as a minister and politician.

His first revelation stunned the Dáil. On taking up office in December 1994, he told the Taoiseach he had availed of the tax amnesty. His own party had severely criticised the controversial qualified pardon for tax evaders when it was introduced by the previous Fianna Fáil/Labour government in 1993. He added, '... in so far as I was aware, all my tax affairs were up to date and paid. I now accept that some of my tax obligations are still outstanding ... I understand that, as people who make the law, politicians have a special responsibility to adhere to the letter of the law.' Lowry said the only political contribution he ever received from Ben Dunne was £5,000 before the general election in 1992. He insisted that the money spent on his house was not a loan, a gift, or a handout, but income, and that he had never intended it to be a tax evasion measure. He said that after 'numerous enquiries' there were 'two other references' to his business in the Price Waterhouse Report. 'The payment of £50,000 was income payable to me under my arrangement with Dunnes Stores and on which tax has been paid. The sums of £6,000 and £6,500 were paid as bonuses by Dunnes Stores for the staff of Streamline Enterprises, not including me. Those payments were made in cash, without deduction of tax.'

It later transpired that the £6,500 was not a bonus, but repayment for money he claimed to have spent. He also neglected to mention three other payments, all in sterling, of £25,000, £40,000 and £40,000. Neither did he tell the Dáil of other bonuses paid to him. However, one passage of his speech, was as astonishing as it was reckless, foolish and dishonest, 'I did not make a secret of the fact that Dunnes Stores paid me for professional services by way of assistance toward my house. If someone were trying to hide income, would he or she not be more likely to put it in an off-shore account?'

This wasn't just one of his casual little fictions; it was a whopper. He had two off-shore accounts in the Isle of Man. One in his own name at Bank of Ireland (I.O.M.) into which £25,000 sterling was lodged in October 1990. The other account was held by Badgeworth Ltd, an Isle of Man registered company he owned, into which £40,000 sterling was lodged for him on 1 August 1991.

However it was another account held in the name of Michael Lowry and his three children in a subsidiary branch of Allied Irish Banks in Jersey which was potentially ruinous. It was opened on 3 September 1991 with a deposit of £100,000 sterling, of which £34,100 sterling was a cheque from Dunnes Stores payable to his company, Streamline Enterprises. It isn't known if Lowry included his off-shore assets when he took advantage of the tax amnesty in 1993, but sources close to Lowry later said it was the account in Jersey which could destroy him. A house he had bought for £150,000 in Blackrock, County Dublin, in September 1996, for which no mortgage was registered, was sold in a panic on 21 January 1997, before the £40,000 refurbishment had been completed.

If he had breached the terms of tax amnesty, Lowry could be facing a mandatory prison sentence. Sections 9, 10 and 11 of the legislation stipulate that if someone availed of the amnesty, but didn't declare all of their hidden income as part of the settlement, they would be liable to a 'fine and a mandatory prison sentence, the term of which cannot exceed eight years.' Section 10 specifically states that where the amnesty has been abused or ignored, there is no mitigation.

Tax specialists said that keeping Lowry out of jail if he had made a false declaration could hang on a Supreme Court ruling to decide if the amnesty legislation is so harsh it is unconstitutional. Then there was probably evasion of income tax and breaches of VAT codes which could bankrupt him. And if he was declared a bankrupt, he couldn't continue as a TD. But for someone who had been confidently predicting his early return to government, Michael Lowry had a more urgent problem: He had lied to the Dáil.

Rumours and gossip in and out of Leinster House, led to the Committee on Procedure and Privilege appointing a retired judge, Gerard Buchanan, on 10 December to report on whether any political parties, members of the Oireachtas, local authorities, state boards, their relatives, or anyone paid directly had benefited from Dunnes Stores. It was, in reality, an examination of the Price Waterhouse report. Judge Buchanan's inquiry was doomed from the outset because it had no authority to subpoena witnesses or hold hearings. Although he submitted an interim report listing payments to politicians, their relatives and a political party on 3 February 1997, it was incomplete. Before he had an opportunity to submit his final report, the Dáil set up a tribunal of inquiry three days later under the chairmanship of Mr Justice Brian McCracken, a High Court judge with formidable intelligence and a specialist knowledge of business law.

The terms of reference were to enquire urgently into ... all payments made by Ben Dunne, Dunnes Stores or any of its associated companies, in cash or in kind, directly or indirectly, whether authorised or unauthorised, to members of the Oireachtas who served between January 1986 and 31 December 1996, their relatives or 'connected persons', and political parties.

A young solicitor, John Lawless of the Chief State Solicitor's office, was appointed to the tribunal's legal team with barristers Denis McCullough, Michael Collins, and Anthony Aston. The registrar was another barrister, Annette O'Connell. The quality of the legal team was a measure of the government's determination to thoroughly investigate the allegations of corruption. The tribunal wrote to every TD and senator who had served between 1986 and 1997 asking if they, their relatives or 'connected persons' had received any money from Dunnes and advertisements were placed in newspapers.

When the tribunal sat in public for the first time at Dublin Castle on 24 February 1997, the chairman made a frank admission. The information available to him was 'almost non-existent'. Mr Justice McCracken appealed for documentation and evidence and promised to protect confidentiality 'in so far as is possible'.

Charles Haughey was waiting and watching the tribunal from Abbeville. He did what he always did when danger threatened: he did nothing. Long experience of crises and scandal taught him to be still and wait, let the enemy come to him. March 1997 marked the fortieth anniversary of his first election as a TD. He had spent his adult life neatly sidestepping the charges of blustering politicians and bureaucrats with the *élan* and arrogance of a matador. His survival as leader of Fianna Fáil for more than 12 years and four terms as Taoiseach, had given him an intimate understanding of crisis management. He had learned that silence and inscrutability, patience and denial are frequently rewarded; that premature explanations and impulsive reactions invite punishment. Hadn't he emerged unscathed from the Buchanan inquiry?

Occasionally, it paid to acknowledge the undeniable. Yes, Ben Dunne had paid £20,000 to his election campaign fund in June 1989 through his wife, Maureen. His brother, Father Eoghan Haughey, received £2,000 from Ben Dunne to say masses. His son, Ciaran, had received £10,000 personally from Ben Dunne, and his company, Celtic Helicopters, had benefited from bank loans negotiated by Des Traynor and guaranteed by funds held in off-shore accounts. Ben Dunne had made two £1,000 donations in 1987 and 1989 to another son, Sean Haughey TD, toward election expenses. But his father denied ever receiving any monies from Ben Dunne.

The tribunal began a protracted and frustrating correspondence with Haughey. The legal team had few clues: just Judge Buchanan's report which listed payments contained in the Price Waterhouse Report, copies of Dáil debates and newspaper clippings alleging Charles Haughey had received £1.1 million. Knowing where to start was a problem. They struck gold sooner than they dared hope. When they contacted Ben Dunne, his solicitor, Noel Smyth, gave an assurance that his client and himself would co-operate fully, just as they had with the earlier Buchanan inquiry.

Ben Dunne's statement included the four payments totalling £1.1 million he made to Haughey through Des Traynor. It also gave details of the complicated trail designed to move the money through jurisdictions with rigidly enforced confidentiality laws. But the statement gave them a route to follow, and it included the identities of the banks and the numbers of Irish and foreign accounts. Still, they didn't sing the Hallelujah Chorus until they saw a reference to £210,000 Dunne had given to Haughey in 1991.

This raised the stakes: it brought the total amount Haughey had apparently received up to £1.3 million. The network of banks, and anonymous accounts weaving through Britain and Switzerland to the Caribbean and Ireland had given Haughey credible deniability but much more crucial to the inquiry was Dunne's claim that he had personally handed three bank drafts, each for £70,000, to Charles Haughey, in his home.

Des Traynor, his financial adviser, had arranged all his money affairs since 1960. Haughey said he didn't know how or where Traynor came up with the money, but he was a man of the highest integrity, held in high esteem by the business community; actually, he was a treasure and something of a financial genius. Their mutual trust ran so deep that Traynor had authority to borrow money and make major decisions about Haughey's finances without even consulting his client. It was Haughey's secretary who forwarded the bills on to another accountant who paid them from money provided by Des Traynor. Haughey didn't have to concern himself with mundane domestic matters, and rarely even carried cash on his person. He kept vulgar matters such as money at arm's length, and didn't even have a personal bank account.

Traynor died in 1994 and took his, and his clients', secrets to the grave. Charlie the conjuror and his cute assistant Des thought they had perfected the look-no-hands illusion. Haughey's convoluted money trail was designed to withstand tax inspectors and accountants armed with fine-point fountain pens. They hadn't foreseen a sledge-hammer assault from a multi millionaire who had nothing to lose.

Ben Dunne's statement that he had put the bank drafts for £210,000 in Haughey's hand, in Abbeville, when he was a serving Taoiseach smashed a delicately constructed and ultra-sophisticated financial rat run designed to withstand the most intense scrutiny. It was the only direct evidence of Haughey receiving money and Dunne was prepared to swear it under oath at the tribunal.

Haughey didn't reply when a copy of Dunne's statement and a request to explain how some of his debts had been paid from the payments made to him by Ben Dunne. It was sent to him on 27 March 1997. A reminder was sent on 2 April and Haughey replied, '... a careful perusal of these documents on their own does not corroborate the allegations being made against me.' The old fox of Kinsealy was playing cat and mouse with the tribunal blood hounds following the money trail.

Even before the tribunal heard its first witness, lawyers had been retained in the Cayman Islands to make an application seeking access to documents held there. Two members of the legal team had also visited London and instructed solicitors and counsel. They were seeking the co-operation of the courts to issue summonses compelling banks officials to give evidence to the tribunal when it sat there.

The secrets were buried at the end of the money trail, in the Cayman Islands, a British dependent territory and the most affluent of the Caribbean islands. Its natural assets are sea-shells, turtles and coconuts. Its phenomenal wealth is derived from another resource, which is given due reverence: banking secrecy. If the Caymans had been a sovereign state, Des Traynor should have been their honorary consul in Ireland. The Dublin banker and financier regularly visited the capital, George Town, for some 30 years.

While they made few demands for information from companies based there, the Cayman authorities insist on them holding their annual general meetings on the island, which earns revenue for the tourist industry. It was Des Traynor who urged his fellow directors in Guinness & Mahon to form a small investment company there in 1969. A mutual friend recommended that he contact John Furze, a banker from Norwich, who worked with the Bank of Nova Scotia Trust in George Town. On 1 January 1974, John Furze and John Collins, his manager at the Bank of Nova Scotia, went to work at the Guinness Mahon Cayman Trust. From the mid-1970s, substantial deposits were placed in Dublin in the name of Guinness Mahon Cayman Trust.

Although it appeared very complicated, like most clever ideas, it was quite simple: Irish residents could keep an off-shore account in a bank in the centre of Dublin, earning just one-eighth of one per cent less interest on their deposits than they would in an ordinary branch of the AIB. Des Traynor was the link. They sent money to him to deposit, or if they needed money, they rang him and he would arrange for them to collect cash, a bank draft or a cheque. Although it was shrouded in secrecy, it had a fatal flaw: of necessity, records would have to be kept in Dublin as well as in George Town.

In 1974 Padraig Collery joined Guinness & Mahon in Dublin to run the computer systems. He worked closely with the deputy chairman, Des Traynor, and was given responsibility for running 'the memorandum accounts', which was really just a record of the transactions of Irish clients whose money was deposited in the Guinness Mahon Cayman Trust. But the clients' names did not appear in the records, and each customer was known by a code. An exact copy of the records was kept by the bank in the Caymans. The memorandum accounts were so sensitive, only Padraig Collery was permitted to work on them, and only on the instructions of Des Traynor. The records were kept on a system totally independent of Guinness & Mahon's other records on the computer. Padraig Collery was the only person (it isn't known if Des Traynor was computer literate) in Guinness & Mahon who knew the password to get access to the 'memorandum accounts'. Only Des Traynor kept a list of the names in Dublin. Padraig Collery knew only the codes, although he learned the identity of some of the account holders when they contacted him or came to collect drafts. Charles Haughey's accounts were S8 and S9.

In 1984, the Guinness Mahon Cayman Trust was sold to the Guinness Mahon's parent company in London, and a year later it was sold on to a consortium which included Des Traynor, John Furze and John Collins. They sold 75 per cent to the London bank, Henry Ansbacher, the name was changed to Ansbacher Ltd, and subsequently to Ansbacher Cayman.

After Traynor left Guinness & Mahon in 1985, Padraig Collery continued to operate the Dublin end of Ansbacher Cayman on direct instructions from his former boss. In 1989, deposits of some £38 million were held in Guinness & Mahon in Dublin by Ansbacher Cayman. To avoid a sudden shift in capital, the deposits were moved out of Guinness & Mahon over three years and in September 1992, Traynor instructed the Irish Intercontinental Bank to open an account in the name of Hamilton Ross & Co., a company registered in the Caymans and controlled by John Furze.

When Des Traynor died in May 1994, John Furze travelled to Dublin for the funeral. It was his second visit in two months, he was a regular at the St Patrick's day celebration. Like pen pals, many of the mourners knew others intimately, although they had never met. Perhaps Mr Furze referred to him as S8, and Padraig Collery called him S9, when they were introduced to Charles Haughey. John Furze, however, was also engaged in earthly pursuits. He visited Des Traynor's office and either destroyed or removed many of the files. The folder detailing the Dunnes/Haughey transactions was spirited back to their final resting place: the Cayman Islands.

The tribunal team had learned a lot about the Ansbacher Cayman accounts, but their chances of getting the one piece of evidence they needed, the Dunnes/Haughey file, were remote. If it had been a criminal investigation, the Attorney General on the Caymans might have agreed to give them access. But by their own admission, in a letter to Haughey dated 3 April 1997, '... there is no allegation ... that in receiving the money in question (either directly or indirectly) you are guilty of any wrongdoing or any breach of the law. Neither is it being alleged that the money in question was paid to you or for your benefit for an improper purpose or with an improper motive or was received by you for an improper purpose or an improper motive.'

Ben Dunne was the first witness called to give evidence to the tribunal on Monday, 21 April 1997. Though one of the richest men in Ireland, like any street-smart urchin, he knew that saying a civic act of contrition, with deep conviction and self-deprecation, was sometimes the price of survival. He could have been a defendant in a District Court, dressed in his Sunday best. A dark suit, a sober tie and a white shirt contrasted markedly with the backs of his ears which were sun-tanned to the same melanomic mahogany as his pudgy face, which carried the excess baggage of too many jet-lagged late nights. Considering he had just opened a new health club, he was no role model for would-be members. He delivered his evidence in a world-weary rasp that sounded like gravel being crunched under a slamming door. He deferred to the pin-stripe suited lawyers as 'Sir', like Elvis playing a poor-little-rich-boy in a movie. His evidence was a *tour de force*.

He gave Fine Gael a total of £185,000. The tribunal heard him say matter-of-factly that Dick Spring rang him and said there was an 'expectation' that businesses in Tralee would support the Waterworld theme park. Ben said he dispatched his driver with a cheque for £50,000 to Dick Spring. John Bruton visited him at his home and trousered a £30,000 cheque after a cup of tea with Ben and his wife.

It never seemed to cross his mind that giving Charlie Haughey £1.3 million through a complicated money trail was any different than giving £100,000 to Fine Gael through a bank account owned by the general secretary. The list went on: another £30,000 to the party via Alan

Dukes; Jim Mitchell had forgotten he had been given £5,000 to share with John Bruton in 1988. Michael Noonan and his constituency organisation got £6,000; Ivan Yates, £5,000. Sean Barrett received £1,000 back in 1987 and the Fianna Fáil Dublin South West Comhairle Cheantair £6,000 the same year.

When Noel Fox told him Charles Haughey needed a group of half a dozen businessmen to each put up £150,000, Ben wouldn't hear of it. 'I think Haughey is making a huge mistake trying to get six or seven people together ... Christ picked twelve apostles and one of them crucified him.' Apart from a seriously deficient knowledge of the bible, it illustrated his ignorance of, or reckless disregard for, the law. He agreed to give all the money to Haughey and detailed each transaction in evidence. His testimony detailing how he gave the three bank drafts, each for £70,000, to Haughey was pure theatre. Noticing Haughey's hang-dog demeanour, he slipped him the £210,000 and said, 'Look, this is something for yourself.' To which, he said, Haughey replied, 'Thank you big fella.' It sounded like an exchange between a deferential beggar and a philanthropic passer-by.

As he gave evidence, his solicitor, Noel Smyth, busied himself, but occasionally he looked at his client with the same kind of pride and satisfaction a dutiful school teacher would admire a protégé. Ben Dunne said with overwhelming modesty that his walkaround budget for hard luck cases and charitable causes had run to £2 million over recent years. There had been 'a good few occasions,' he said, when he spent up to £500,000 to help people in trouble. It seemed a contradiction that a hard-headed businessman who had built Dunnes Stores into a billion pound company couldn't see that lavishing money on politicians and political parties may be something more than a loss leader.

At times the big man giving evidence could have been a latter-day Elvis, giving cars to buddies and extravagant donations to charities. There seemed to be no end of his generosity-without-commitment. Early in the tribunal everyone agreed that Ben Dunne had neither sought, nor received, any favour from anyone on whom he heaped his bounty. It appeared to reverse one of the natural laws of business – 'There is no such a thing as a free lunch.'

The next witness, a banker from the Isle of Man, Julian Harper, giving evidence of how he routed a £470,000 payment to Haughey through Switzerland, was asked if a particular instruction from Ben Dunne was unusual, 'It would be difficult to say that anything he did was unusual because everything he did was unusual, so it was usual to be unusual.'

Fine Gael's general secretary, Jim Miley, said Dunne's contribution of £185,000 was the largest ever made to the party.

Margaret Heffernan told the tribunal she was 'flabbergasted' when 'Bernard' told her he had given Charles Haughey £1 million and when she asked Haughey twice about it, he was evasive, but suggested her younger brother was 'unstable'.

The first week's evidence ended with a sensation: Ben Dunne's solicitor, Noel Smyth, told the tribunal he had made notes of five conversations he had with Mr Haughey and posted them to himself by registered letter. Smyth asked for a ruling on the confidentiality of his meetings with Haughey and the chairman, Mr Justice McCracken, ruled that Haughey should be allowed to see the contents of the unopened envelope first. He dispatched the solicitor for the tribunal, John Lawless, to hand them personally to Haughey at his home that evening.

The next day the tribunal sat, Monday, 28 April, serious damage was done to Fine Gael, the senior partner in the coalition government. The Taoiseach appeared to conflict with evidence he had given to the beef tribunal where he said that individual party members, including the leader, would not be made aware of donations to the party. He told the Dunnes tribunal the party leader would not normally be made aware of contributions but he was aware of the approach made to Ben Dunne because he had made it.

A succession of government ministers gave evidence to the tribunal of receiving donations from Ben Dunne that day and the evening television news carried damning pictures of shiny black Mercedes' lined up outside Dublin Castle. It looked like a mafia wedding.

A general election was expected to be called in the coming weeks, the tribunal needed to do more leg work on the seemingly never-ending money trail, and Charles Haughey sought limited legal representation on the issue of confidentiality. The chairman adjourned the tribunal for four weeks.

On 18 May, Mr Justice McCracken, senior counsel, Denis McCullough and Michael Collins, and the tribunal's solicitor, John Lawless, arrived in the Cayman Islands. A local lawyer, Charles Quin, from Northern Ireland, who was representing the tribunal, picked them up at the airport. The Irish team was not surprised when John Furze vigorously opposed their application to the courts to get access to his records and they had no reason to be hopeful when the court reserved its decision. The tribunal had uncovered the money trail from Ben Dunne to the Caymans, and from the Caymans to Charles Haughey. But the documentary evidence which completed the circle from Dunne to Haughey was still locked in a safe in John Furze's office.

Michael Lowry had been re-elected to his seat running as an independent in the general election in June 1997 when the Rainbow Coalition government lost power. He had been disowned by the party, but the voters of Tipperary North had not deserted him. Unlike his former ministerial colleagues who had been confident giving their evidence two months ago before the election, he looked dejected and vulnerable sitting alone in the tribunal. He said 'weasel words' had crept into his statement to the Dáil the previous December when he said that if someone was trying to hide income, wouldn't they put it into an off-shore account? He insisted 'on oath' that he was not trying to mislead the Dáil with his statement. His house, which cost Dunnes Stores £395,000, was a 'modest house of good standard' which had since become a tourist attraction.

As he sat in the witness box Lowry seemed to be hearing echoes of testimony Ben Dunne had given to the tribunal earlier, 'Certainly when it came to Mr Lowry as to tax, I would believe then and would believe now that Mr Lowry is old enough and mature enough to be able to take care of his own tax problems, and I wouldn't have been involved in anything like that.'

Lowry said his life had been a nightmare for the previous eight months. He had 'tried and tried and tried' to regularise his 'unsatisfactory financial arrangements' with Ben Dunne. His failure to do this had been the source of 'all the anguish, distress, strain and misery' he had endured. He assured the tribunal that Ben Dunne had sought no political favours. Later, the chairman said he was satisfied that Lowry's motive in accepting the personal payments, and entering into an arrangement where he would be paid bonuses personally, was to enable him to evade tax. Mr Justice McCracken said Lowry, '... operated his businesses on two levels, one level through the company, which made a small profit and duly paid its taxes, and on a second level whereby large sums of money would be paid to him personally in a clandestine manner.'

Mr Justice McCracken said that the threat of disclosure had left Lowry open to blackmail, and continued, '... perhaps the most damaging aspect of this relationship, is that there could be a public perception that a person in a position of a government minister and a member of cabinet was able to ignore, and indeed cynically evade, both the taxation and exchange control laws of the State with impunity.'

He concluded, '... it is an appalling situation that a government minister and chairman of a political party can be seen to have been consistently benefiting from the black economy from shortly after he was first elected to Dáil Éireann. If such a person can behave in this way without serious sanctions being imposed, it becomes very difficult to condemn others who similarly flout the law.'

Chapter Fourteen

Charles Haughey was still waiting and watching, but now he was worried: from where he stood, the barbarians were at the gates of Abbeville. The media had been snapping at him like hyenas circling a wounded old buffalo since the payments to politicians scandal had broken the previous December. Plausible deniability was never a realistic option; survival was now his only ambition. Haughey had always been a serial denier which is just a few fibs short of a compulsive liar. Some of his most loyal friends found it odd that he would almost automatically deny anything. He even denied the most innocuous sighting of him in a public place where they had seen him themselves. It could be a cynical ploy too, a percentage call for a populist politician: when his honesty was questioned, he knew nothing he said could convince his enemies; but even the most incredible denial gave comfort to his devotees. Some of his admirers thought his apparently pointless and transparent lies were more of an eccentric idiosyncrasy than a character defect. Still, it was a strange quirk for a Taoiseach: amateur psychiatrists put it all down to the perjury at the Arms Trial.

Since the tribunal had first sat in February, he denied receiving any money from Ben Dunne or Dunnes Stores. His legal team was not obliged to believe he was telling the truth. Private judgements would never interfere with their professional obligations. They were bound by his instructions and he kept insisting to them that he had received no money from Ben Dunne. More than a generation previously he had been through a high octane trial, denied everything, and emerged to confound his tormentors. But times had changed: the odds and the evidence were heavily stacked against him this time.

It was his word against Ben Dunne's. He was a former Taoiseach who had saved his country from bankruptcy ten years before; he had been responsible for some of the most innovative legislation since independence; walked the international stage with the leaders of the free world. He had left public life quoting Othello, 'I have done the State some service; they know't: No more of that.' Ben Dunne was a drug addict with a penchant for call-girls whose own family believed he was unfit to run their business and that he was possibly mentally unstable. If it had been a jury deciding who was telling the truth, Haughey may have shaded it. The prospect of Noel Smyth, a successful solicitor and a family man who took his religious duties seriously, supporting Ben Dunne's evidence and contradicting him, changed everything. Haughey and Smyth had held clandestine meetings and shared secrets, and there were notes of their conversations ....

After he had helped Ben Dunne prepare his statement in March, the tribunal's legal team asked Smyth to make a statement. It posed a problem: he had had five meetings with Haughey and if he included the contents in his statement, the details would become public. For a start, he would be obliged to give an account of the meetings and it would be unfair to Haughey who wouldn't have an opportunity of knowing their content in advance. Smyth was also concerned that Haughey might deny having any meetings with him, or claim that he tried to bribe him with £1 million.

The day before the tribunal had its first public hearing on 21 April, Smyth spoke to his legal team and explained his dilemma to them. His two senior counsel, Seamus McKenna and Paul Gallagher, and Brian Murray BL insisted he had to make a full and complete statement. Smyth said he had to find a way of protecting the sensitive passages, particularly the fact that when he brought him copies of the bank drafts, Haughey suggested to him that they were an embarrassment because they had been lodged in Des Traynor's account in the Irish Intercontinental Bank.

Smyth called his secretary into the office that Sunday to type the statements: one detailing the facts and the information he had uncovered about the banks and accounts; the other dealing with his private meetings with Haughey. He arranged to meet counsel in his office at 7.30 the following morning. Smyth suggested handing them to the tribunal in a sealed envelope; counsel said the tribunal wouldn't accept it. Then he came up with the answer: he would put the statements into an envelope, seal it, and address it to the judge, then put that envelope into another envelope, seal it, address it to himself and send it by registered post. His staff were alerted not to open the envelope when it was delivered to his office and it was put in a safe with the postal receipt.

Smyth knew he was going to be called as a witness and when he was, he could alert the tribunal to the existence of the envelope. However, Smyth would insist on being directed by the tribunal on the question of the confidentiality of his meetings with Haughey. He had been sensitive about confidentiality because he felt Haughey might have told him things he wouldn't if Smyth hadn't been a lawyer. It caused a commotion on Friday 25 April when Smyth told the tribunal he had made notes of five conversations he had had with Haughey and posted them to himself. When the question of confidentiality arose, Mr Justice McCracken ordered that the envelope should be be sent, unopened, to Charles Haughey. The envelope contained the silver bullet evidence that forced Haughey to face up to the truth.

Haughey had been handed the envelope by the tribunal's solicitor, John Lawless, at the door of Abbeville that Friday evening. When he read Noel Smyth's notes, he consulted his legal team and the following Monday he decided to seek limited representation at the Tribunal, solely on the question of confidentiality. However, when the leader of his legal team, Eoin McGonigal SC, looked for an adjournment on Monday, 28 April, Mr Justice McCracken said the tribunal wouldn't be sitting again for another month. Haughey had borrowed more time, but he was overdrawn on credibility.

Veteran Haughey watchers said that while he was a brilliant tactician, the former Taoiseach was a useless strategist; he could plan the next couple of moves with inspiration, but ingenious short-term solutions would inevitably cost him the game. His handling of the Noel Smyth notes problem vindicated this view of him.

The adjournment on 28 April gave Haughey nine weeks to study Noel Smyth's version of the five meetings and prepare his own statement which he had delayed delivering to the tribunal since March. He had never given a satisfactory reply to 70 letters sent to him by the tribunal. But no amount of time would change the bald fact that Noel Smyth's notes totally contradicted his own denials and supported Ben Dunne's testimony that he had given him £1.3 million. Desperate circumstances dictated a resolute response and he devised a final solution to the tribunal problem.

Maybe it was his FCA training that inspired his strategy of a legal pincer movement. On Monday, 7 July, he would give the tribunal the detailed statement it had been seeking since 7 March; and within an hour, he would destroy the tribunal. He had decided to take out McCracken. It was vintage Haughey playing by Big Boys Rules, which basically means there are no rules.

A single telephone call would have told him that Brian McCracken was among the brightest on the High Court bench. Formidable forensic skills, a nimble intellect and a mastery of detail had taken him to the top of his profession. He was also genuinely modest, pleasant and unfailingly polite which warped judgement could interpret as 'an easy mark'.

Just before the tribunal sat at 10.30 a.m. on Monday, 7 July, Haughey's long and detailed statement was delivered to the tribunal along with the envelope containing Noel Smyth's notes. There wasn't sufficient time for them to examine Haughey's statement and they still couldn't open Smyth's notes until their status had been decided in the tribunal.

When the hearing began, there was some surprise when Eoin McGonigal SC said Noel Smyth's conversations with his client were private, but an issue of confidentiality didn't arise. Neither Mr Justice McCracken nor his legal team could have known what was planned when McGonigal said that the tribunal would have to consider if Smyth should now be a party to the proceedings in his own right. In retrospect, it was the first indication that Haughey regarded Ben Dunne's solicitor as a player: Noel Smyth was to be the vehicle used to deliver the knockout blow to McCracken. The chairman asked Smyth if he objected to his statement being shown to the tribunal; he had no objections. Mr Justice McCracken adjourned the tribunal for 24 hours, to give his own legal team and the others an opportunity to read the statements which had just been delivered.

Eoin McGonigal, an experienced and authoritative senior counsel, approached Denis McCullough SC, the leader of the tribunal legal team, and his colleague, Michael Collins SC. He told them that his client, Mr Haughey, was very concerned about Mr Justice McCracken's position. There was a real danger that a person for whom Mr Justice McCracken had acted for personally was going to give evidence that would potentially conflict with testimony given by his client.

When he was a barrister, Brian McCracken had one of the busiest chancery practices in the Law Library. He was a man of the highest integrity and was much sought after to act in complicated business cases. In the past, he had been instructed by Noel Smyth's firm of solicitors, but then he had also been briefed by Pat O'Connor, Charles Haughey's long-time friend and solicitor. In practice, it would be almost impossible in such a small country for any successful barrister not to have been instructed by most of the leading firms of solicitors.

However, he had represented Noel Smyth personally at the inquiry into the Johnston, Mooney and O'Brien site which was sold to Telecom. He had appeared for Smyth in the High Court on matters arising from the inquiry which had been ordered by the then Minister for Industry and Commerce, Des O'Malley.

McGonigal stressed that there was no suggestion that Mr Justice McCracken would be anything less than scrupulously fair and impartial. But justice must not only be done, it must be seen to be done. Mr Justice McCracken could find himself in an invidious position if Noel Smyth's evidence contradicted Charles Haughey's and he had to decide which of them he should believe. Problems could arise if someone else questioned his impartiality.

It was normal practice for a judge to stand down if they believed there was a potential conflict. On the first day of the High Court hearing of Ben Dunne's challenge to the Dunne trust in November 1994, Mr Justice Murphy's first address to the court was to say that he had previously acted for Frank Dunne and asked if anyone had objections. No one did, and he continued to sit, but the case was settled before any evidence was given.

If Mr Justice McCracken asked the tribunal if anyone objected to his chairmanship because he had once acted for Noel Smyth, it seemed almost certain that Haughey would seize the opportunity to ask him to disqualify himself.

The tribunal's legal team went to consult Mr Justice McCracken, but it is understood none of them thought he should stand down. If he did, there may be a public perception that he had somehow done something wrong which would be grossly unfair to a decent and honourable High Court judge. If he didn't, his findings at the conclusion could lead to judicial reviews, appeals and litigation which would ultimately undermine the work of the tribunal. But either way, a controversy would have had enormous repercussions far beyond the cloistered legal establishment.

The payments to politicians scandal was one of the biggest political upheavals in the history of the State and it had dominated the news for nearly nine months. Reports of the hearings were followed with great interest and events in the tribunal had been regularly commented on and debated on radio and television. McCracken had won unstinting praise for his handling of the proceedings from both the public and politicians. It was universally agreed that a thorough investigation of the allegations of corruption was essential to restore the confidence in the political system. Opinion polls reflected the public's cynicism and politicians had never been held in such low esteem.

If Mr Justice McCracken did stand down, the tribunal's six months work would have to be abandoned at enormous financial cost. But there may be a higher price to be paid: it would almost inevitably excite public outrage and provoke a political crisis.

No one outside Mr Justice McCracken, Haughey's and the tribunal's legal team knew of the deepening crisis in the hours after the tribunal was adjourned that morning. The tribunal's legal team spoke to Noel Smyth and explained their difficulty. The notes of Smyth's conversations with Haughey, which were only delivered to the tribunal that morning, did not give the dates when the meetings took place. When the notes were studied and analysed, the tribunal team interviewed Smyth again and Mr Justice McCracken made an order of discovery on Noel Smyth's diaries and telephone logs and asked Smyth to swear an affidavit.

Everyone in Smyth's office in Fitzwilliam Square was working on the discovery notice, checking the phone logs and diaries. As part of his office procedures, every phone call to Smyth's office was logged, dated and timed and he kept a diary of all his appointments. As well as the five meetings, there were dozens of telephone calls from Haughey between December 1996 and February 1997 which were omitted from Haughey's statement. And they retrieved details of Smyth's mobile phone calls to Haughey from old Telecom bills. Then they saw the evidence that would destroy Haughey: Smyth's diaries and telephone logs proved he had been in regular contact with Haughey in 1994. In particular, his accompanying affidavit would confirm he had called to Haughey in March 1994.

When Haughey's legal team arrived at the tribunal on the Tuesday morning, they were unaware that an order of discovery had been made on Smyth, and that he had made a third statement. After consultation with their client, the legal team's task that morning was to follow Haughey's apocalyptic instructions and make a formal application to the tribunal to request Mr Justice McCracken to remove himself as chairman.

Before they went into the tribunal, Haughey's legal team were given copies of Smyth's new statement, his telephone logs and diaries. It stopped them in their tracks: just when they were about to deliver a mortal blow to the tribunal, Smyth's new evidence totally destroyed their client's credibility. The shock and anger was reflected in Eoin McGonigal's face when he stood up to speak, 'This morning I have been furnished with new documents which were not available to me before this time and I require a short adjournment to enable me to take full instructions in relation to the information.'

New information? Coming after the mysterious and unexpected adjournment the morning before, the other legal teams and the press and public galleries were astonished and bewildered at the suggestion of important new documents and information. Their curiosity was further excited when the chairman said, 'Well, Mr McGonigal, do you realise that [that] information was only in the hands of the tribunal this morning as well ... I understand you might want to take instructions ...'

Nobody except those who were there know what words were exchanged between Haughey and his legal team that afternoon. Whatever was in Smyth's new statement so profoundly contradicted the instructions Haughey had given his legal team, they must have told him they could no longer act for him. Haughey had been lying to them and it would be ethically impossible for his lawyers to continue to act for him if he continued to mislead them.

On the Wednesday morning, the tribunal began with Eoin McGonigal reading a statement from Charles Haughey, 'I wish to thank the chairman for yesterday's adjournment. As a result of reviewing the excellent work of the tribunal in considering the very helpful documentation recently received from Mr Ben Dunne's solicitor, I now accept I received the £1.3 million from Mr Ben Dunne and that I became aware that he was the donor to the late Mr Traynor in 1993 and furthermore I now accept Mr Dunne's evidence that he handed me £210,000 in Abbeville in November, 1991. In making this statement, I wish to make it clear that until yesterday I had mistakenly instructed my legal team. They have however agreed to continue acting for me for the duration of the tribunal. I wish to thank them in this regard. I will give evidence to the tribunal when required to do so.'

It was nothing less than an unconditional surrender. Haughey had admitted receiving the £1.3 million and he accepted that he had been handed the three drafts for £210,000 by Dunne at his home and because his evidence no longer conflicted with Noel Smyth's, the question of Mr Justice McCracken standing down, didn't arise.

Haughey must have hoped that a successful challenge to the chairman and the subsequent collapse of the tribunal would have left his own statement something of an academic curiosity. Although he did have the benefit of Noel Smyth's notes for nine weeks when he prepared his first statement, it could never have been convincing. Since the tribunal began, he had, effectively, been calling Ben Dunne a liar. Now Smyth was supporting Dunne's evidence, and worse: he was exposing the former Taoiseach as a liar.

After he had made a frank admission of his guilt on Wednesday, the statement he had delivered to the tribunal on Monday was shown up as a master stroke of cynicism and deceit. The tumultuous events and his subsequent admission, meant that his original statement was never read out to the tribunal. At lunch on Wednesday, the distinguished High Court judge who Haughey had tried to oust by suggesting he may have a conflict of interest, had two directly contradictory statements from Haughey delivered to him within 48 hours of each other: one protesting his innocence, the other confessing his guilt.

In his statement delivered on Monday, Haughey had flatly contradicted Smyth's version of the meetings. He explained his relationship with Des Traynor, described his meetings with Margaret Heffernan, and for the first time accepted that 'the payments totalling £1.3 million ... were received for my benefit.' But there was a caveat, 'I had no knowledge of the circumstances surrounding the payment of such monies, but I accept the description as offered in evidence to this tribunal by Mr Noel Fox insofar as it touches on the four payments totalling £1.1 million.'

He went on to dispute Ben Dunne's evidence that he had personally handed him three bank drafts of £70,000 each. Dunne was mistaken, said Haughey, he wasn't aware of their existence until Noel Smyth referred to them on 3 February, at one of their five meetings. He went on to explain that he had first met Noel Smyth when Smyth, Dunne and their wives had dinner with him in Abbeville on 9 October 1992. The drafting of the details of his five meetings with Smyth between December 1996 and February 1997 was as disingenuous as it was dishonest.

Haughey said that Smyth had telephoned him around the time the Lowry story broke the previous December and asked if he knew who had leaked the details. He didn't know, and he told Smyth that: 'whoever is responsible was playing a very dangerous game' and arranged to see him on Saturday, 12 December 1996. Smyth insisted they meet in a neighbouring house to Haughey's where he showed him a copy of the Price Waterhouse Report and pointed out that there was no mention of himself, although his wife Maureen, his son Ciaran and brother Eoghan did appear in it.

They met at the same house, 'Emsworth', on Saturday, 4 January at 11 a.m. and discussed the possibility of a tribunal of inquiry being set up and and its possible consequences. In his statement, Haughey said Smyth telephoned him on the morning of 3 February and said he had three bank drafts in his possession which, Smyth said, Ben Dunne believed he handed to Haughey. He knew nothing about them and invited Smyth to meet him in Kinsealy that afternoon. When he arrived, Smyth showed him photocopies of the three drafts; Haughey said he had never seen them before.

The statement went on to deny most of the details in Smyth's notes. Haughey said Smyth had not asked him if he had lodged the three drafts to his own account, nor did he (Haughey) say they could be a source of considerable embarrassment. Nor did he indicate that the drafts may have been lodged in Des Traynor's account. He denied asking Smyth to get rid of, or destroy the copies of the bank drafts. Smyth, he said, had not informed him that Ben Dunne would be obliged to inform the tribunal that he had given him the three bank drafts.

Haughey's original statement referred to a meeting in Abbeville later in February 1997, when Smyth had advised him to take the easy way out and tell the tribunal that the payments from Dunnes through Traynor had been for his benefit. He said that Smyth had told him Ben Dunne was prepared to provide £1 million to cover his tax liability. Haughey rejected the offer 'out of hand'. He was particularly sensitive to one point and said, 'I have never spoken about my place in history or the community or anything of that kind to anyone.' He did recall one part of the conversation where Smyth asked him if he had availed of the 1993 tax amnesty 'and I informed him that I had not'.

In Wednesday's statement, when Haughey finally put up his hands in surrender, he included a sarcastic reference to Noel Smyth. He attributed 'the very helpful documentation recently received from Mr Ben Dunne's solicitor' to his acceptance that, 'I received the £1.3 million from Mr Ben Dunne'.

There hardly seemed much point in Smyth delivering his testimony after Haughey's confession, but his evidence was put on the record. However, the solicitor's minimalist and matter-of-fact delivery to the tribunal did not convey the tense atmosphere that must have permeated the meetings. At times, Haughey's study in Abbeville could have been Vito Corleone's constituency clinic. Most of the people who came to see Haughey were in trouble, or seeking business advice and he occasionally sorted out delicate domestic matters. But even when he was young, Haughey was the wise man whom others feared. He always demanded, and was usually given, respect. Back in 1994, he was in his seventieth year, with a lifetime of triumph and struggle behind him, he was faced with a young, abrasive solicitor who had the edge on him. Smyth was not intimidated by Haughey's omnipotent persona, he had more corporate scalps on his belt than most litigating lawyers. Smyth was clinically looking at the facts; Haughey was looking at his place in history. And the notes Smyth had prepared for the tribunal and posted to himself were a basic chronological record of his meetings with Haughey, but they didn't fill in the detail of those extraordinary encounters. They were pure theatre.

They were never friends, but Charles Haughey invited Noel Smyth to his house that afternoon in March 1994 when he telephoned and said he had something important to discuss. When the solicitor arrived, Haughey brought him into his study at the front of Abbeville and allowed him do the talking. Smyth explained that Ben Dunne was taking a legal action to challenge the Dunne trust and that he had just returned from Hong Kong and the Isle of Man where he had been retrieving documents for the proceedings. He came to the point of their meeting quickly: the documents showed that £1.1 million had been paid to him, and Ben Dunne intended using the information in his evidence. Haughey denied receiving it, but Smyth had the documents that proved the money had been paid and Ben Dunne's evidence would be that it was intended for him.

The meeting took place two years after he resigned as Taoiseach, he had avoided controversy, lived quietly, and even his old enemies were mellowing towards him. He was a political pensioner, no longer a threat. Haughey rang Smyth before he left for Cheltenham races a couple of weeks later and invited him to breakfast at seven o'clock the next morning. His horse, Flashing Steel, was running in the Gold Cup and he should have been on top of the world but he was agitated and nervous and said he thought Smyth and Dunne were trying to destroy him, that he had been in public life for years and it would be devastating if the legal action were to proceed. He was concerned that the documentation naming him would be in the hands of strangers, and when more than ten people were involved some of them would be certain to be his enemies. Smyth told him there was nothing he could do, that he was bound by a discovery order and promised to keep him informed. Haughey called him again on 22 March and again on 24 March. On 15, 19 and 25 April; some 20 times in 1994 and Smyth had rung him just as often.

Smyth rang him a week after Ben Dunne settled his case with the trust on 19 November, and he was invited out to Abbeville for a celebratory drink. Haughey rang him again after he received a letter from Dunnes Stores demanding the return of their money and invited Smyth to discuss it at Abbeville. He wanted an assurance that Ben Dunne wouldn't appear as a witness for Dunnes Stores if they came after him for the £1.1 million. Smyth told him he didn't believe Dunnes would issue proceedings against him because it would reopen the controversy with Ben they had just paid £125 million to close.

In early December 1996, when the story about Michael Lowry and Dunnes Stores hit the headlines, Smyth called Haughey again and asked if he knew who was leaking the story. They met in person for the first time since 1994 in Haughey's neighbour's house, 'Emsworth', on 4 December. Haughey was concerned about an inquiry into payments to politicians and if Ben Dunne would give evidence to it. Smyth told him his client was unlikely to appear, he had enough of litigation.

The next time they met, again in 'Emsworth', it was to discuss the Buchanan inquiry which was set up to examine the Price Waterhouse Report. Haughey only relaxed when Smyth opened a copy of the report and showed him that his name didn't appear in it. Smyth explained that his name only appeared on the Notice of Particulars for the Dunne trust case. Haughey was relieved, almost cocky again. Smyth urged caution; Haughey said lawyers were always pessimists. He reminded Haughey of the Telecom scandal and how a departmental inquiry turned into a High Court inspection. If Buchanan didn't come up with answers, public anger would demand a tribunal of inquiry. He cautioned Haughey that his name was included in the in 1994 trust case and showed him the documents where it indicated he had received £1.3 million.

By the beginning of February, it wasn't a question of whether there would be a tribunal of inquiry but how quickly could it be set up.

Smyth rang Haughey and called out to see him on 3 February 1997, with photocopies of the three drafts. He asked him if Ben had given them to him; Haughey said they could be a source of embarrassment: they had been lodged into Des Traynor's account in the Irish Intercontinental Bank. Smyth said that the three drafts linked Haughey to all the other payments. Haughey told him that he was going to deny everything. Smyth said this was different. A person would stand up in a tribunal and say, 'I gave them to him'. If Haughey continued to deny it, it would be pointed out to him that the drafts ended up in an account directly related to the rest of the payments. Ben Dunne had told Smyth he remembered handing the three bank drafts to Haughey at Abbeville. Smyth asked Haughey if he had availed of the tax amnesty, because if he had included the earlier payments in his declaration, his tax liability might only have been around £200,000. Haughey said he hadn't.

In late February, when the tribunal was already underway, Smyth rang Haughey and was invited to Abbeville. He told Haughey that Ben had understood how serious the situation was for him. The best thing

Haughey could do at that stage was say he was heartily sorry he had taken the money, but when he took it he had been mixing with Thatcher, Kohl, Bush and other world leaders. Smyth said that if he told the truth and told the Irish people that he couldn't be seen with 'no arse in his pants' being chased by the ACC bank, they would understand. That he needed the money to pay off his debts and always had it in the back of his mind that he could sell off his property to repay the loan; Smyth told him to do a *mea culpa* on it.

Smyth told Dunne about his meeting with Haughey and Ben asked what it all meant. 'It means now, unequivocally, that he's gone.' Dunne asked what his main problems were. Tax, replied Smyth. He explained that the money Dunne gave Haughey would be deemed to be a gift and there would be tax, interest and maybe penalties. Smyth reckoned Haughey's tax bill would at least be £1 million. 'Does he have it?,' asked Dunne. Smyth said no. Dunne said he'd give him the million pounds. Smyth urged caution and said Haughey would probably take the money, that Ben's chances of getting it back were remote and it would be messy. Ben Dunne asked his solicitor what his position would be if Haughey took the £1 million. Smyth advised that it would vindicate him, put him in a situation where everything he said would be 100 per cent correct. Then Haughey could tell the tribunal that he had been to the taxman and paid him £1 million. Ben told Smyth that Haughey didn't need to say where he got the £1 million from.

Smyth asked Haughey if he would get a good tax lawyer or accountant and go to the Revenue Commissioners, he could then speak to the tribunal's legal team. He told Haughey the tribunal was an ideal forum to tell his story, that they weren't interested in a crucifixion, their job was to get the truth. It wasn't a judgemental tribunal and it had no penal powers. Haughey said he couldn't do that. Smyth told him not to make any hasty decisions, that this was a golden opportunity to solve his problems. Haughey said it would lose him his place in history. Smyth said he understood how important that was, and that he had given all his life to public service. Smyth said it was way beyond that now, that we now live in an age where people are suspicious of power, that younger people are running the country. He said the new generation didn't know him or what he had done. All they know is that this politician with a grandiose lifestyle has a huge pile of money that he got in unacceptable circumstances. No one had ever spoken to Haughey like that and it must have been particularly galling for him to be put in his place in his own home.

Smyth rang a few days later and Haughey confirmed that he would not accept the £1 million. When Smyth told Ben Dunne, he was instructed to withdraw the offer: he didn't want Haughey coming back when the going got rough at a later stage and saying he'd like to take up the offer. The million pound offer was made while Ben Dunne was preparing his statement for the tribunal and it included details of the £1.3 million payment to Haughey.

In his evidence to the tribunal, Noel Smyth said there was an element of panic in Charles Haughey's reaction when he asked him to confirm that he had received the three bank drafts from Ben Dunne. The former chairman of the Revenue Commissioners, Philip Curran, confirmed in evidence that when he was Taoiseach, Charles Haughey asked him personally to meet Ben Dunne and discuss a tax problem related to Dunnes Stores. However, Dunne didn't seem to know what he wanted when they met and Philip Curran asked him to write it down and he would ask his staff to see what, within the law, could be done. He didn't hear from Dunne again. When Ben Dunne gave evidence for the second time, he repeated that he had neither sought, nor received, any favours from Haughey. He said his £1.3 million gift was a charitable act, although Haughey had never mentioned it to him, let alone thanked him. 'Looking back with hindsight,' said Dunne, 'I suppose I'd call it odd.'

Ciaran Haughey told the tribunal he had no knowledge of £150,000 from the Ansbacher deposits to repay a 'soft loan' from Dunnes Stores to his company, Celtic Helicopters. He said Des Traynor had organised what he believed were four 'ordinary commercial' loans for Celtic Helicopters between 1991 and 1993.

Of all the scandals to emerge from the tribunal, the revelation that Des Traynor controlled £38 million held for Irish citizens in the secret Ansbacher Cayman account from his office in Dublin was profoundly shocking. The individual depositor's money was pooled in the Caymans, then the combined fund was put on deposit in Guinness & Mahon bank in Dublin. The interest earned on the deposits was just one-eighth of a per cent less than normal rates and the individual account holders were identified by a code, from S1 to S9. Charles Haughey's accounts, one in sterling, the other in Deutschemarks, were coded S8 and S9. The great advantage was that no one in Ireland, including the Revenue Commissioners, knew the identity of the depositors or the balance of their accounts; no one except Des Traynor.

When the Ansbacher Cayman scheme was exposed, there was a public outcry about rich and privileged people evading taxes and flouting exchange control laws with impunity. Mr Justice McCracken said it would be ethically improper to extend the terms of reference of his inquiry to examine the Ansbacher Cayman accounts. He revealed that people had given the inquiry information in confidence and added that from the information available to him, Charles Haughey was the only politician to have benefited from the Ansbacher deposits.

After he had taken the oath, Charles Haughey read another statement to the tribunal. 'Chairman, I accept that I have not co-operated with this tribunal in the manner which might have been expected of me. I deeply regret that I have allowed this situation to arise. When I walked out of Government Buildings on February the 11th, 1992 I was determined to leave public life firmly behind me, to detach myself completely from it, and to leave those following me free to manage things in their own way, without any attempt by me to influence or interfere.

The effect of this transition has been that my recollection of events became remote and confused. In endeavouring to recall times, dates, the sequence of events and details of meetings and conversations to the tribunal, I have been at this disadvantage. I omitted to instruct my lawyers fully. It is against this background that I sent correspondence to the tribunal and in particular my letters of the 7th of March 1997, 3rd of April 1997, my statement of the 7th of July and counsel's statement to the tribunal on the 30th of June 1997. These letters and statements were unhelpful to the tribunal in the carrying out of its work.

I was concerned as to the effect that the publication of these payments would have for me in the public mind and, in hindsight, I accept that a lot of the problems and embarrassment that I have caused would have been avoided if I had been more forthcoming in each and every relevant period.'

The statement went on to reiterate that he known since late 1993 that he had received £1.3 million from Ben Dunne, but he was never aware of it while he was in office. Mr Dunne didn't seek, nor was he granted any favours, he said, nor was there any improper motive associated with the payments. He apologised to Mr Justice McCracken, to the tribunal's legal team, to all concerned, but he emphasised that, '... this serious lapse in the management of my personal affairs did not in any way affect the discharge of my public duty when in office'.

When he finished reading his statement, Haughey sat back, composed himself, and fixed his gaze on the counsel for the tribunal. Denis McCullough SC was not the partisan inquisitor Charles Haughey's enemies would have chosen to satisfy their bloodlust and Haughey's opponents easily out-numbered his supporters in the public gallery in King George's Hall on Tuesday, 15 July. McCullough's mellifluous baritone began the examination, 'Mr Haughey, I appreciate the candour of your statement, and I'm sure it's not been easy for you to make it, but you have covered a certain amount of ground that lies between us, but I'm sure you will appreciate that I must ask you some questions notwithstanding your statement, and I intend to do so.'

Denis McCullough gift-wrapped his tough questions in a soft voice and courteous manner. His job was to elicit information rather than satisfy prurient interest and a desire for revenge. His gentle probing revealed that when he was Taoiseach in the late 1980s, Mr Haughey's salary from the State, including his ministerial pension, was £53,810. But McCullough pointed out that his living expenses and domestic overheads came to £705,000 between 1988 and 1991.

'My private finances were perhaps peripheral to my life. I left them to Mr Traynor to look after,' said Haughey. '... I'd just like to make a point that I didn't have a lavish lifestyle. My work was my lifestyle ... when I was in office, I worked every day, all day. There was no room for an extravagant lifestyle.'

McCullough probed gently, '... I think Mr Traynor told you [in mid 1993] that Mr Dunne had paid for your benefit £1.3 million; is that the position?'

'Yes.'

'Before that time, Mr Haughey, are you saying that it never occurred to you to ask Mr Traynor where the money was coming from?'

'That's correct.'

McCullough's dry wit occasionally broke through, particularly when Haughey seemed close to suggesting Des Traynor obtained money for him from the tooth fairy.

'But as an accountant yourself, Mr Haughey, did you ever wonder where he was getting the money?'

'No, and I must say ... at that stage I was a very acquiescent accountant, I hadn't known the accountancy world for many decades.'

'But while you may not have been an accountant for some time, you had been Minister for Finance.'

The tribunal erupted in laughter. Haughey nodded *touche*, turned toward the bench and said: 'Mr Chairman, I think an accountant often makes a very bad Minister for Finance.'

Later, McCullough asked him, '... monies were paid in a very circuitous way to bank accounts which were operated for your benefit in a very complicated and elaborate way. And that would indicate that it was intended that no one should ever find out about the payments by Mr Dunne to you?'

'That is a fair conclusion, but I would like to say that I didn't know anything about those bank accounts or that trail which the tribunal has established,' replied Haughey.

McCullough asked him if he sat in Abbeville waiting to see whether the tribunal would gather sufficient evidence to make it incumbent on him to make a statement.

'Well ... I suppose basically I was looking at the face of disclosure.'

McCullough continued to press him, '... was there not a hope and the belief, Mr Haughey, that the tribunal would not be able to uncover this hidden trail of payments?'

'Not really.'

'... I suggest to you, that it was not until the tribunal had presented the evidence to you prior to the 30th of June that you decided to make a statement?'

'Yes.'

'And you still contested on the 30th of June that Mr Dunne handed any monies to you personally?'

'Yes.'

'Mr Haughey, as recently as the 30th of June and the 7th of July, you were still persisting in accounts of events which were short of the truth?'

'I was reluctant to face the disclosure of the situation.'

'So what you said in your statement as recently as the 7th of July was untrue?'

'Incorrect.'

'Untrue,' insisted McCullough.

'If you wish to use that word, yes,' said Haughey.

'I'm afraid I must, Mr Haughey.' Denis McCullough didn't need to call him a liar. He had simply allowed Haughey's circumlocutory obfuscations to ridicule themselves and expose his naked dishonesty.

Haughey finished giving evidence at 12.30 p.m., stood down from the witness box and went to a room to prepare for his exit. Rather than take a back door and avoid the crowds which were filling the courtyard at Dublin Castle, he had decided to leave by the grand entrance to the State Apartments. A member of staff was dispatched to tell the media he would be leaving at 1 p.m. Camera crews, reporters, photographers and curious onlookers gathered in anticipation.

Bang on time, Haughey emerged from the gloom of Dublin Castle into the sunlight. Always a stickler for punctuality, he expected the same from others. He looked very pleased with himself. Presumably when he went to his room after giving evidence, his retinue had told him he had performed magnificently in the witness box. Well they would, wouldn't they? They always did.

As Haughey stepped out of the door, some of the crowd surged forward cheering and he gave a regal wave in Pavlovian response. Then a chorus of boos drowned out the applause and there were shouts of 'lock him up' and 'liar'. He paused for a about a second, looked puzzled, then shook hands with the leader of his legal team, the long-suffering Eoin McGonigal SC, and was ushered towards the front passenger seat of the waiting State car. Frank Harrison, a septuagenarian waiter, rushed forward, pushed a security guard aside and firmly clasped Haughey's hand. The crowd was more curious than aggressive and, after the car sped Haughey away toward Abbeville and ignominy, they remained huddled in groups. After 40 years in public life he hadn't lost it: they will be talking about him for a long time ....

Epilogue

An opinion poll taken three days after the publication of the McCracken tribunal's findings, showed that nearly 90 per cent of the electorate believed Charles Haughey and Michael Lowry should go to jail if convicted of breaching tax and exchange control laws. An overwhelming 89 per cent said the former Taoiseach should be prosecuted and 87 per cent believed the former minister should face criminal charges for their roles in the payments to politicians scandal. The poll, conducted by Irish Marketing Surveys for the *Irish Independent*, also showed that 77 per cent of those interviewed wanted a second tribunal of inquiry set up to investigate decisions made by Haughey and Lowry during their terms in office since 1986. More ominous, was the finding that 79 per cent were convinced that business and political 'cosy cartels' existed, and nearly two out of every three voters (62 per cent) believed that financial corruption was widespread among TDs. The public's vote of no confidence in serving politicians was probably inevitable after the publication of the tribunal's findings on Monday, 25 August 1997.

Mr Justice McCracken was scathing: he said that Charles Haughey's attitude to the tribunal might have amounted to an offence under section 1(2) of the Tribunal of Inquiry (Evidence) Act and sent the relevant papers to the Director of Public Prosecutions to consider prosecuting him. The tribunal had been unable to accept much of Haughey's evidence, particularly his assertion that he wasn't aware that monies were held for him in Ansbacher Cayman. Mr Justice McCracken said he couldn't believe that Haughey was not aware of the money or of the tax implications for receiving £1.3 million from Ben Dunne. He maintained that Haughey deliberately 'shrouded the gifts in secrecy and allowed the money to be kept off-shore in an attempt to ensure that the revenue authorities would never know of the gifts ....'

He continued, 'It is quite unacceptable that a member of Dáil Éireann, and in particular a cabinet member and Taoiseach, should be supported in his personal lifestyle by gifts made to him personally. It is particularly unacceptable that such gifts should emanate from prominent businessmen within the State. The possibility that political or financial favour could be sought in return for such gifts, or even be given without them being sought, is very high, and if such gifts are permissible, they would inevitably lead in some cases to bribery and corruption.'

Mr Justice McCracken went on to say there was no evidence of any favour being sought of Haughey by Ben Dunne, the Dunne family or the Dunnes Stores group, or no political impropriety by Haughey in relation to the gifts, although '... that does not take away from the unacceptable nature of them.' He also censured Dunnes Stores, 'It was clearly unwise that one person (Ben Dunne) should be given such unsupervised financial control over the affairs of a business the size of the Dunnes Stores group, and as a matter of general principle the company must have some responsibility for the actions of an officer to whom it delegates such wide powers.'

The system of payment by Dunnes Stores to Michael Lowry was designed to assist him in evading tax, and it was an 'appalling situation that Mr Lowry consistently benefited from the black economy from shortly after his election to the Dáil. There was an 'unhealthy business relationship between Lowry and Dunnes Stores which was 'particularly disturbing' because he was a cabinet member and chairman of the Fine Gael parliamentary party. Mr Justice McCracken added that there was no political impropriety on the part of Lowry and he never sought to intervene in any way on behalf of Dunnes Stores.

The tribunal went on to make recommendations, in particular that politicians making false declarations under the Ethics in Public Office and Electoral Acts, should face criminal prosecution and be banned from membership of the Dáil or Seanad. Mr Justice McCracken said that the sanctions under the two Acts, which call for the disclosure of gifts, campaign contributions and a register of the financial, property and other interests of politicians, 'do not go far enough.' He recommended that the powers of the Ombudsman be extended, and his office should have the authority to demand the production of documents and be able to seek documents and witnesses in other countries. In a reference to how his legal team had obtained information on the Ansbacher accounts, he said, 'This tribunal found these powers to be extremely beneficial in its investigations.'

The combined effect of the Ethics in Public Office Act 1995 and the Electoral Act 1997 amounted to a 'commendable attempt' to ensure there was no repeat of the 'unacceptable elements' of the financial transactions in which Haughey and Lowry were involved. These acts would be highly effective in monitoring 'ordinary political donations', said Mr Justice

McCracken. But the two Acts did 'not go far enough' to deal with payments made to off-shore accounts under a veil of secrecy. The system of disclosure of interests required in the Ethics in Public Office Act is 'open to abuse'.

He said that a proposal by Fianna Fáil requiring bankers, accountants or other professional advisers to disclose any unusual or large accounts, was not practical and unlikely to be particularly effective. Mr Justice McCracken said that if a member of the Dáil or Seanad was not going to comply with the rules of the Ethics or Electoral Acts, they would not comply with obligations to register payments. 'A person who goes to such lengths to deceive the Revenue authorities (about off-shore accounts) and the public, will almost certainly to go equal lengths to deceive the Oireachtas.'

After the findings were published, Charles Haughey was the subject of some of the most vituperative and sustained criticism ever made of any serving or retired politician in the Republic of Ireland. Michael Lowry's reputation was in ruins too, but he was pleased that Mr Justice McCracken's findings supported his contention that there had been no political favours sought or given in his relationship with Dunnes Stores.

Although he maintained a stoic public silence, Haughey privately insisted he had not been handed the three £70,000 bank drafts by Ben Dunne in Abbeville. It was the only direct evidence of him physically receiving money. The other four payments, totalling £1.1 million, had been made to Des Traynor and Haughey consistently said he had no knowledge of how they were paid or the route the money followed. Although he accepted that the £210,000 (and the other £1.1million) had been for his benefit, he was adamant that the three drafts were not handed to him at his home in November 1991. It did seem odd that Haughey was concerned about this one allegation: it was like someone complaining about being wrongly convicted of double parking when they had confessed to dangerous driving.

Sources close to Haughey said that Mr Justice McCracken had been inaccurate where he said on page 65 of his report, that in his statement on the 9 July 1997 '... Haughey acknowledged that he had personally received the three bank drafts from Mr Ben Dunne.' Haughey's 9 July statement actually said, '... I now accept Mr Dunne's evidence that he handed me £210,000 in Abbeville.' In his own evidence to the tribunal on the 15 July, Haughey said, 'I have no recollection of that meeting, but I believe that on the facts as presented, I have no alternative but to accept it.' Using his own famously Jesuitical approach to syntactical analysis,

Haughey seemed to be saying was that while he had no alternative but to accept Ben Dunne's evidence, he did not believe Dunne handed the drafts to him.

Ben Dunne handed the three drafts to someone in November 1991. Three years later, in documents for his legal case against the family trust in November 1994, he said he had given them to his siblings. In his evidence to the tribunal on 22 April, he said: 'They [the drafts] weren't drawn for the benefit of Mr Haughey. They were drawn for a personal thing, nothing to do with politicians. He still believed they were given to his siblings up to December 1996, and only realised he had given them to Haughey when he saw bankers' book evidence. Dunne was quite certain of that when he gave evidence to the tribunal on 22 April, '... in earlier proceedings I did think I may have given them to other members of my family and *on bankers' book evidence which I saw*, it transpired that I didn't give them to my family.' In evidence, Dunne also said that he thought the drafts were for someone other than Haughey until he 'got the information from the Irish Intercontinental Bank.'

However, Ben Dunne's solicitor , Noel Smyth, told the tribunal on 25 April that there was *no bankers' book evidence*. The mysterious bankers' book evidence was supposed to have been obtained on a discovery order made by Noel Smyth on the Irish Intercontinental Bank where the three £70,000 drafts were lodged. When he was asked if he had got the discovery order, Smyth said '*No*, because this case, this procedure had been initiated at the dying days of the original controversy with the family [in November 1994]; and therefore, when the case was settled I didn't pursue it further.' In a later question, Smyth was asked if he went back to the Irish Intercontinental Bank, and he said '*No*. That morning Mr Dunne said "I think that's wrong", I think those drafts were never given to the family" and I said "Well, who got them?" and he related the story about playing golf and that he had the drafts in his pocket. And I said, "Well, you know that's the first time I heard of this particular instance" ... his explanation was that he now, having considered the matter, believed that he had given them to Mr Haughey.'

Smyth's testimony directly contradicts Ben Dunne's evidence. Dunne told the tribunal on 22 April that he changed his mind and only decided he gave the drafts to Haughey after he saw the bankers' book evidence. Noel Smyth's evidence on 25 April was an unequivocal: 'No', he didn't get bankers' book evidence on discovery from the Irish Intercontinental Bank where the drafts were lodged.

There is no doubt that the drafts were lodged by Des Traynor's secretary for Charles Haughey's benefit, in the Irish Intercontinental Bank, on three separate dates in November and December 1991. According to his evidence, from November 1991 Ben Dunne believed he had given the drafts to his family until he saw bankers' book evidence some time in December 1996. If there was no bankers' book evidence, as his solicitor swore on oath, what did change Ben Dunne's mind after six years?

Both Haughey and Lowry believe they were caught in the crossfire of the ongoing battle between Ben Dunne and his sister Margaret Heffernan. They have a point: if the details of Ben Dunne's payments to politicians hadn't been listed in documents prepared for his litigation against the family trust in 1994, it is extremely unlikely the financial chicanery of Haughey and Lowry would have been exposed. Clearly Ben Dunne had no compunction about using the potential scandal of his payments to Haughey in his legal battle with his family but neither Haughey nor Lowry can complain about being used as cannon fodder in an internecine war. If they took the money, they must take the consequences. If a politician, particularly a Taoiseach or a member of a cabinet, takes solicited and secret payments from the richest family in the country, they are at the mercy of whoever has bought them. Haughey and Lowry shamed themselves, their families and the profession of politics.

The Dunne family's legal battles, like blood feuds, seem to have an interminable shelf life. At the time of writing, mid-November 1997, the Supreme Court has reserved a judgment on their latest legal wrangle. Margaret Heffernan has appealed an order granted to her brother Ben to remove her as executrix of their sister Therese's estate. In April 1997, the High Court appointed a Dublin accountant, to administer the estate worth some £22 million. Mrs Heffernan had been named by Therese to be the executrix of her will before she died unexpectedly in September 1995. Ben Dunne said that Margaret Heffernan failed fundamentally in her duties as executrix, particularly about an affidavit to the Revenue Commissioners about the value of Therese Dunne's 265 preference shares in the Dunne Group of companies. In the High Court, Mr Justice Smyth said Mrs Heffernan, as executrix, had sworn an affidavit for the Inland Revenue in which the 265 shares were returned at a value of £1 each. Mr Dunne's solicitor had claimed his client was concerned the shares had not been returned at their correct value. Mr Justice Smyth said he was not concerned about the value of the shares. Mrs Heffernan contended the correct valuation of the shares had been made to the Inland Revenue and that, even if it was wrong, it was none of her brother's business. Mr Justice

Smyth said Ben Dunne appeared to have felt so frustrated and excluded from what he considered his legitimate concerns, that in June 1996, he had issued legal proceedings. The administrator was appointed after what Mr Justice Smyth said was 'the unspoken but clear antipathy of the litigants towards each other.'

It can't be just a row about money since Ben Dunne and Margaret Heffernan are two of the richest individuals in the country. Although, like the politicians who had become paid-for possessions, a sister's probate seemed to become be a substitute for throwing crockery in an ongoing family row.

Dunnes Stores continues to thrive as the country's most successful retailers and Margaret Heffernan and Frank Dunne are in an apparently unassailable position at the head of the family business.

Meanwhile Ben Dunne is building his chain of health clubs, one of the fastest-growing segments of the leisure industry in Europe, and he has bullish plans for the future. A 'Wellness Centre', as the owner described his £6 million venture, is in Blanchardstown in the north west suburbs of Dublin. An old adversary, Albert Gubay, has a rival fitness centre nearby, and after he opened in June 1997, Dunne offered Gubay's customers a week's free usage of his centre. Old competitive habits die hard. He has plans to develop another centre in the south of Dublin and add a full health screening service for his members. He is also preparing to launch a chain of hotels. 'The standard will be four or five star, but they will be much cheaper than the existing hotels in that category,' he told business journalist Des Crowley. 'We have, of course, talked to people, but we are not going into partnership. I have had two partnerships in my life. My marriage has succeeded but my partnership with Dunnes Stores failed.'

Then there's Michael Lowry, who, after suffering personal and political disgrace, faces financial ruin and possibly prison. Sources have intimated that Michael Lowry may be looking to Ben Dunne for further financial help as he faces into another tribunal of inquiry. After his re-election as an independent TD for North Tipperary in June 1997, he was severely criticised in the report of the McCracken tribunal and his fall from grace was even more more dramatic than his vertiginous rise to success. Unlike Haughey who had enjoyed a rollercoaster ride through life before he was finally derailed at the age of 72, Michael Lowry was yesterday's man before he was 44 years old.

Noel Fox, a trustee of the Dunne's family trust and a senior partner in Oliver Freaney & Company, auditors to Dunnes Stores, was to be the focus of an investigation into any professional or business misconduct by accountants named in the McCracken tribunal report. A former Supreme Court Judge, John Blayney, was appointed to head the inquiry set up by the Institute of Chartered Accountants in Ireland. Noel Fox was the go-between who spoke to Ben Dunne after he was contacted by Des Traynor when he was seeking financial help for Charles Haughey. In April 1995, Margaret Heffernan told the tribunal that Fox had failed to disclose to her, or the other directors, that her brother, Ben, had redirected more than £1 million of the company's money to Haughey. It was suggested that Fox had a conflict of interest between his role as a trustee and his position in Oliver Freaney & Company, auditors to Dunnes Stores and Streamline Enterprises, Michael Lowry's company. Haughey, who became a Fellow of the Institute of Chartered Accountants in Ireland in 1955, is also likely to have his conduct investigated by the inquiry.

There would be another tribunal to examine the decisions both Haughey and Lowry had taken in government and their financial affairs. The government approved the appointment of Mr Justice Michael Moriarty as chairman of the tribunal and the first public hearing was held at Dublin Castle on 31 October 1997. However the terms of reference laid down for the Moriarty tribunal exclude an investigation of the source of funds in the Ansbacher Cayman accounts, unless it can be proved they were used to fund politicians. On 11 September 1997, the Fine Gael chief whip, Sean Barrett, told his colleagues in the Labour Party and Democratic Left, that his party would not be supporting demands for an investigation into the Ansbacher Cayman accounts. Although Irish citizens held £38 million in the secret off-shore accounts, and there was strong circumstantial evidence of tax fraud, Michael Noonan, Fine Gael's finance spokesman, said a full investigation would be a 'prurient trawl through the private affairs of decent citizens.' Noonan said, 'If one says that we are to examine private citizens' Ansbacher and Guinness Mahon accounts, the law of equity, in my view, would make it necessary to examine every bank account held in any kind of off-shore arrangement. That might have unforeseen effects on the economy.' Government ministers were also saying privately that an investigation of the Ansbacher Cayman accounts could have an adverse effect on the Irish economy.

Maybe it was scandal fatigue, perhaps they knew it would be difficult to get access to information about, and confirm the identity of, the depositors. Probably they were not prepared to look into the off-shore accounts for fear of who and what they would find there. The tribunal of inquiry into payments to politicians found senior members of both Fianna Fáil and Fine Gael, the country's two largest political parties, had flagrantly flouted the law. After the biggest political scandal in a generation, the government and the largest opposition party, have drawn a line in the sand of the Caribbean.

Index